To Patty!

Towards fulfillment &

Your eternal happiness

& Joy!

Dr. Z

25 Days to
Living Your Happiness

Dr. Zayd Abdul-Karim

ISBN: 978-1-4834-4527-4 (sc)
ISBN: 978-1-4834-4526-7 (e)

Lulu Publishing Services rev. date: 02/09/2016

What Others Are Saying

"Extremely powerful concepts made simple and easy to apply the knowledge. We are given a practical way to change our behavior using spiritual concepts."

"I hope people will embrace the concept of moving away from an ego based life--it is a painful way to live and it turns people away from you instead of towards you...because of your book, I am aware of the ego based behavior in me and others...I am a changed person because I read this book!"

"I am honored that you have shared this wonderful book, **25 Days to Living Your Happiness.** It is already making a great deal of difference for me. The book and the author are Amazing."

"...By the way, this week, you may not realize it, but you had a great impact on me through these daily exercises. Each day just by focusing on the day's theme I have come through so many rough moments better than before."

"Dearest friend, Zayd, thank you for a wonderful contribution to my life...I am allowing myself to be present with each behavior and new habits are magically expanding...My spirit is just opening up and for this I am forever grateful. And your spirit is helping my happiness grow!"

"The praise is to God, I am having great experiences AND things are getting a whole lot better. Glory to God, being really works. It's very powerful. I didn't even have to do anything." ☺

"Every so often a gift shows up at a time when one is seeking peace – peace of body, peace of mind, and ultimately peace of spirit. Dr. Zayd's book **25 Days...** showed up at a time in my life when peace seemed almost inconceivable. My ego was shouting for me to continue to "do" more because if I didn't I would fall behind, I would ultimately fail."

"Once I got into it and started from day one, it seemed to be a natural progression. Intuitively, I felt that beginning with selfless, there is no better way to start than looking at yourself...The reading was such a very high energy."

"This book has helped me change focus from "not another thing," to get into spirit. One can't walk around always in a spiritual way, at first maybe. This book can help you divert yourself away from ego. Ego has an energy that pulls you. I've used the concepts to pull me into spirit mode. I really feel blessed that I have it."

ADDITIONAL RESOURCES BY
DR. ZAYD ABDUL-KARIM

Conversations with Mother Leadership

Legacy of Extraordinary Leadership for Community Life

Seven Self-Leadership Practices to Freedom and Power

7 Steps in Deep Transitions: A Spiritual Guide to Peace of Mind, Prosperity, and Success

DEEP TRANSITIONS: Jump Starting Your Business

With G-d's Name
The Merciful Benefactor
The Merciful Redeemer
All Praise belongs to the Giver of Life
The One Who Has Power over All Things

Love to All

In Gratitude and Service

TABLE OF CONTENTS

PREFACE

"25 *Days to Living Your Happiness"* is the conscious application of simple Laws that are universal. Readers become participants in a self-motivated course of improvement and joyous living. I find this book to be in accordance with the Divine Plan of Creation, meaning that it is wholly constructive in its approach; introduces the individual to their unlimited power and potential; takes the individual beyond the daily routines of labor and turmoil; and gives each active participant tools that will bring them more permanent happiness, productivity, and overall success.

Each moment of life is an opportunity to create Perfection. *"25 Days to Living Your Happiness"* helps to make those opportunities evident. That which is real does not change. What the reader gains through this book are applications of Universal Laws that have everlasting effects.

For those seeking their True Purpose in Life, this program is a path that leads to the 'causeless cause.' Participants will begin to live and give for the shear joy of it. What Dr. Zayd has accomplished is a major step for humanity's progress in a world of constant change, challenges and limitations. He truly provides the tools for any reader to see the magnificent opportunities offered in Life's Journey.

I am particularly pleased with the daily affirmations. The word 'I AM' is the most powerful word we can ever use. It conveys the feeling of acceptance of conditions within and around an individual whether they are constructive or not. Expressing oneself through constructive words, phrases and behaviors is a Key entry point to self-mastery.

– Stanley El

Stanley El is the Founder and President of The National Society of American Business Owners and publishers of 'Wealth Creation' ™ magazine. He is the nation's authority on 'American Business Ownership Development' ™, host of 'The American Dream' radio show broadcasting weekly on Rowan Radio 89.7 WGLS-FM in New Jersey, and a commentator on the Higher Laws of Law.

Introduction

Everyone wants to be happy. Some people look for happiness in external things. The more possessions they attain, the more happiness they perceive. There is a bumper sticker that reads: "The one who dies with the most toys wins." I'm not sure if that statement is true. However, everyone is entitled to their own perspective. For me, happiness is not related to external, material things. I believe happiness comes from within, and only from within. There are many people who earn a lot of money and have many possessions, yet, they are not happy. Something is missing in their lives. Something from within their soul, heart and mind is missing that keeps them from being happy.

What if you could deliberately project your energy on a daily basis and invite people and happenings in favor of your happiness? Would you commit yourself to doing what was required? This book is written to help you connect with your inner self and find, practice, and live your happiness.

After eight years of research with training participants and reflections on my own human experiences I've reached a few conclusions. First, it appears that a person's ego based in fear, doubt and worry are great contributors to unhappiness. Second, it appears that happiness is a concept related to the abstract world of spirituality. Third, contrasting values, beliefs and attitudes of a negative ego (fear) and a positive spirit (love) carry certain energies that will manifest in physical form, eventually. Fourth, there are concrete ways to move toward development of your soul or "higher self" on a daily basis. These conclusions are outlined throughout the book.

This book offers a brief discussion on how ego and spirit can show up in everyday interactions through attitudes, feelings, and behaviors. This introduction is a foundation to clarify the concepts and how they may apply in your life. The remainder of the book offers you daily reading and exercises to focus your attention, energy, and "points of attraction" in the spiritual direction. The love energies of spirit outlined in this book are ordered in a progressive manner from lowest to highest. By being aware of these energies and the progressive scale, you can change attitudes and behaviors to create greater happiness.

Before publication, six persons agreed to "do" this book as "research participants" and offer their reflections as data as a validation of these techniques. Some of their thoughts and feelings are written toward the end of selected chapters, under the heading "Experiences in Spirit." Also, I've included notes from my journal as I "did" the book with them. Thank you to all research participants. I've excluded their names to protect them from exposing personal information in their comments.

Methodology

The method for applying this information is reading one chapter, doing the exercises, and writing a journal entry each day. Through this process you will be moving with and attracting more positive energies. Consequently, you will be living more of your happiness. Each day you'll experience growth in strength and intensity. After 25 days you will have created new habits for yourself in a positive direction.

There are at least three ways to use this book. One way is to start at the beginning and read one chapter per day. Another way is to identify where you are on the scale of contrasting energies at any given moment, and focus on that chapter (reading and exercises) for that day. For example, if you are feeling frustration, then you could focus on the day of patience to change your 'vibration.' Third, you could allow yourself to be guided by opening the book to any page and do the reading and exercises for that day. Whichever way you choose to use the book, be consistent for at least 25 consecutive days. This is an exciting adventure where you will be led by Spirit!

As you do your daily reading and exercises, you are encouraged to keep a written journal to track the changes that occur in your thoughts, feelings, attitudes, behaviors and results. Or you could use a tape recorder to record your thoughts daily. Either way it's important to keep a record of your experiences.

Finally, if you want to make the positive changes a more permanent part of your life, then I am encouraging you to continue using this process over the next 100 days. In other words, commit yourself to repeating the 25 day process four times; reading each day and doing the exercises. You could also focus on one quality and repeat the affirmations and exercises, for that one energy, over for a 7 day or even 30 day period,

Concepts of Spirit and Ego

What do human beings know of spirit? The knowledge of spirit given to us is only a little. The human capacity to understand the spiritual or non-physical world is too limited. We cannot fully comprehend the vastness and power of the spiritual world. All of the books written and speeches given on this topic are reflections of the interest in spirituality. However, recognize what is available to you is a very small of amount of knowledge on this aspect of life, the non-physical/spiritual world built on faith.

With that being stated, this writing looks at the experiences of human beings and the contrasting energies that evolves from concepts of a diseased ego, with the personality or the lower part of self; and concepts of what I call Soulality, the human spirit or the higher self. I don't say my views written here are right. I just say this is how I see it. I trust your intelligence to make up your own mind.

Over a three year period, I asked training participants: What shows up in attitudes and behaviors when people bring their ego to you? Some of the responses received are listed below and categorized as Lower Self/ Personality-Ego:

Being Selfish	-	Desiring Control	-	Blaming
Finding Fault	-	Being Judgmental	-	Expressing Guilt
Seeking Approval	-	Being Rigid	-	Behaving Arrogantly

Being Critical	-	Complaining	-	Exhibiting Superiority
Being Defensive	-	Resisting what is	-	Exhibiting Inferiority
Worrying	-	Feeling insecure	-	Being complacent
Being ungrateful	-	Feeling self-doubt	-	Envying and Jealousy

These ego responses are based in FEAR, DOUBT, and WORRY. The diseased ego is afraid it will lose the attention in the moment. It is afraid it will be ignored. Sometimes fear shows up as Fear of Failure, Fear of Rejection, Fear of the Unknown, Fear of Success, etc. Any of these fears are like a big bowl filled with garbage. When "eaten" the mind, heart and soul is impacted negatively. Once the fear is digested, the ego-based attitudes, feelings and behaviors show up. What do notice about these ego-based terms? They are all negative. Likewise, the energy coming from them is negative.

Certainly, some degree of fear is healthy. The mortal fear is fear of losing one's physical life. It makes sense to fear walking out in front of a car traveling 70 miles per hour. Even more important is the fear of displeasing our Guardian Creator who sustains life. This type of fear comes from a sense of worth, obligation and excellence. We want to live up to the human excellence G-d put in us and expects from us.

However, the fear we're talking about in this book can be unhealthy and dominate one's life. These energies are ignited by the kinds of questions the ego asks such as: What's in it for me? What do I get? How does it make me look? A self-centered perspective begins to dominate every interaction through thoughts and feelings which lead to behaviors and results consistent with the negativity.

Additionally, I asked the same question regarding spirit: What attitudes and behaviors show up when someone approaches you from their spirit? The responses are listed below and categorized as Higher Self/Soulality.

Spirit:

Desire to Serve	-	Acceptance of what is	-	Defenselessness
Responsibility	-	Self-approval	-	Happiness
Trust	-	Courage	-	Learning
Patience	-	Kindness	-	Freedom
Humility	-	Flexibility	-	Joy
Passion	-	Gratitude	-	Appreciation

These qualities of spirit can be wrapped up in the word LOVE. When a person is operating from love many of these positive perceptions and attitudes show up. They tend to attract people and positive outcomes to you. The questions spirit asks are: How can I help? How can I serve? How can I contribute to make things better?

Scale of Contrasting Energies

As I continued this inquiry with people over the years, I began to see these two sets of answers as distinct energies. For example, consider the energies as cause and the outcome as effect; by putting energy into "x" as the cause, then "y" is the effect. I concluded that energies are points of attraction. Similar to what we put our energy into; we attract whatever we put our attention on. The two columns of contrasting energies and points of attraction have been written below as a chart. They are not meant to be an all inclusive list of ego and spirit energies. However, they do convey the contrast between some ego-fear and spirit-love based perspectives.

CONTRASTING ENERGIES &
POINTS OF ATTRACTION

EGO	–	SPIRIT
Judgment	–	Mercy
Punishment	–	Forgiveness
Pain	–	Joy
Sorrow	–	Happiness
Constraint	–	Freedom
Conflict	–	Peace
Motion	–	Stillness
Noise	–	Silence
Frustration	–	Patience
Devaluation	–	Appreciation
Attachment	–	Detachment
Aggression	–	Surrender
Control	–	Acceptance
Holding Tightly	–	Letting Go
Dissatisfaction	–	Contentment
Rigid	–	Flexible
Victim	–	Responsible
Powerless	–	Hopeful
Difficult	–	Ease
Doing	–	Being
Past	–	Present
Isolation	–	Connection
Domination	–	Communication
Selfish (I, Me)	–	Selfless (Others)

The following chapters provide brief discussions on both the ego energies/points of attraction and the corresponding energies of spirit. By putting your attention on one spirit energy each day, for the next 25 days, you will shift your points of attraction and develop new attitudes and behavioral habits. Enjoy the journey and be aware of what shows up in your life as a result of refocusing your attention.

Today I Serve Others Unconditionally

Selfish or Selfless Service?

These two contrasting energies are written at the bottom of the table. Although the ego is created good in its natural, healthy state. The word "ego" in this writing refers to the diseased ego based in fear, doubt, worry, and selfishness. On the ego side, the first word is selfish. What is selfishness? It is an energy focusing on "me, myself and I." From the ego perspective, the individual is the only thing that is important and exists. The ego mind is mostly concerned with itself. We see this with people who think and say words like: "What's in it for me?" "How is it going to make me look?" "What do I get from it?" "Why would you do this to me?" "This always happens to me?" "I deserve better than this?" I, I, I and me, me, me. Those ideas of selfishness, "I"ness, and "Me"ness focus on what "I" want to get, what "I" need to get in order to feel better about myself. "I'm not good enough yet." "I am incomplete." "I need more." At the bottom left side of the table of contrasting energies, there is no place else to go but over to selfless service and upward to Mercy. This will make you begin to feel better. Or you can choose to stay in the left side energies starting with selfishness and go deeper into negativity toward judgment.

Selfishness brings more selfishness. When using selfishness, one can never feel complete because the focus is too narrow. The diseased ego operates as if it's the only thing that exists in the world. Then it becomes the center of attention; the center of one's view. This translates into self-centeredness, self-absorption, and self-consumption.

There is a part of being human, that requires some selfishness to a degree. You are here to accomplish certain things. You are here for a specific purpose that's known only to you. Up to a point, selfishness

DAY 1

requires that you take care of yourself before you can take care of others. However, what we're examining is how selfishness takes on a life of its own and grows. Eventually, it overpowers the human being and becomes so dominant in the life that nothing else exists except the perspective of "I" and "Me." "I must be right." "I am the only thing that exists and if you don't fall in my view of the world, then there is obviously something wrong with you." This is the selfish perspective.

The other side spirit focuses on others and "We." How can we give service to others? We use a term selfless, although it's not totally self less or soul less, but it is less focused on the "I" and the "me." It is more focused on the "you" and "others." It's about being willing, focusing and having your thoughts, images, and emotions on how you can serve other people. As a result, you'll ask questions like: How can I help? How can I serve? Certainly "I" is in the statements, but it's really a question of how can we serve? How can we help? How can we make things better? What can we be and do that works toward the good? Continuous improvement is the goal. This notion of selflessness and otherness expands into a focus on ONENESS. Awareness that everything is part of the ONE and there is no separation. This is a spiritual perspective.

When you give service to other people, you are really serving yourself. When you help someone else, you are really helping yourself. This viewpoint becomes expansive because it includes everything; every living creature. It includes things that we can't see and hear. It's all part of the service. It includes inspiration. It includes motivation. It includes a number of positive attitudes. Therefore, service becomes all-inclusive.

For example, when you are involved with others you have a sense of accountability. You are committed to some type of service. Then you are motivated to do more, often times, to keep that commitment of service to others. Many of the great teachers and leaders throughout history have demonstrated selfless service – Mahatma

Ghandi, Dr. Martin Luther King, Jr., Mother Theresa, Imam Warith Deen Mohammed and countless others whose names are unknown. They focused on others in their service and contributed greatly to human kind.

This we call selfless service: a focus on others, a focus on contribution as opposed to the ego perspective that's only focused on the "me" and what I'll get. Therefore, that type of energy is all about getting and taking. On the other side, spirit is focused on giving, sharing, partnering, and collaborating towards the good.

The ego selfishness seems to work towards a good, but the good is limited. Because the good only exists within the mind of ego as a selfish, limited, narrow view. What it wants is the only good that exists in the moment. Whereas there is a larger good, a universal good that spirit tends to serve when our focus is on others.

Experiences in Spirit

Zayd's notes: "After writing the affirmation 15 times, the words seemed etched into my mind. Throughout the day I found my mind repeating those words inside. When interacting with people I seemed to be consciously looking for opportunities to give some service such as holding the door open; giving a dollar; and allowing others to go first while walking or driving. I feel good as my behavior matches the affirmation. There is a positive energy in knowing I am doing what I declared I'd do for the day."

One participant reported: "The reading, especially this one was such a high. It was a very high energy. Today, I got a call from my sister in Atlanta. She is having problems with her son who is diagnosed with A.D.D. At the moment she called, I really wasn't ready to take a call. But, my reading kicked in. I shut down all that I was thinking about and had to do. I said: 'let me consciously listen and really serve her at this point.' I felt good that I got that practice in and it just came naturally. I didn't have to seek it. Today's lesson heightened my awareness, consciousness of really focusing in on service. What helped the conversation was listening and only responding when she asked for a response."

Another research participant wrote: "I feel like this exercise had lots of potential. I also feel like I was seriously challenged to be true to the affirmation. It didn't turn out as expected, but I was constantly reminding myself mentally and emotionally that I was at their (my family's) service. I just made myself available. I felt a difference in the way my mother responded to me. She was a lot more calm than usual probably because she didn't have to ask me to do things. I was just doing them."

Actions for Today:

1. Write this affirmation 15 times:

   I am service unconditionally

2. With every person you meet today ask them: How can I help you?

3. When you answer your telephone today say: "Thank you for calling. This is <u>your name</u>. How can I help you today?

4. Identify at least two people you can serve today (spouse, child, relative, coworker, friend, etc.). Contact them and ask: "How may I help you today?" Then follow through to give them the service they want.

5. At the end of the day, reflect on any lessons that you learned.

6. Write down your thoughts and feelings about your experience in a journal.

DAY 2

Today I Communicate Openly With Others

Domination or Communication?

The next contrasting energies are domination (ego) and communication (spirit). What is the energy of domination? It can be defined as force. It is energy of overpowering with force; exerting one's own values and will onto someone else or in a situation. This could imply an unawareness of others perspectives, strengths, and viewpoints because ego, as domination, is only concerned about its own ways. In domination, ego is forcing its selfishness.

For the diseased ego there is no other way except its own. It has a logic, namely that it should dominate the situation. For example, let's say an individual is in a learning situation at school, work, or family and in their ego view they disagree with someone. The desire to dominate could show up as a dispute, an argument or at the very least a strong expression that they disagree. Is it possible their ego's need to dominate encourages them to express that disagreement verbally, nonverbally, and/or emotionally? It's ok to disagree, but it doesn't have to be expressed. One can disagree and not be disagreeable. Also, what does disagreement have to do with learning? Do we have to agree with each other in order to learn? No. If a diseased ego is dominating the energy of an individual, then over time that attitude may be expressed in some type of dominant behavior.

Many people are living from ego energies. Some people love to see dominant behavior. A prime example is in the athletic arena. In professional, college, and high school sports, the athlete who is valued the most is the one who dominates the competition. The one who is able to score at will or make dominating plays is viewed favorably.

In sports and business the team that dominates in all aspects of the game wins. Sometimes domination is expressed between individual teammates. We've seen athletes on the same team physically fight each other when their ego is out of control. In business situations, have you ever seen a team member who wants to dominate the conversation? They want to make sure their view is expressed at every point during the meeting. They don't want to let go because ego's goal is to win.

Domination becomes a win-lose practice. If ego wins then you lose. If ego loses then you win. This approach perpetuates itself. No matter how much the individual dominates, the diseased ego always wants to dominate more.

Domination leads to more domination because these energies are based in the fear "if I don't dominate this situation, then I'll lose." That's the ego perspective motivated by fear, doubt, worry and selfishness. This is in sharp contrast to the spirit energy around communication.

Communication is a two-way process that focuses on shared understanding and meaning. It's okay to have a different viewpoint with communication because the goal is understanding. The essence of the communication process is to engage in dialogue where an individual wants to understand another persons' point of view. Communication is first understanding the other person's needs and interests before seeking to be understood. Focusing on the other person and seeking to understand them first, creates a field of openness. This usually involves processes of questioning and expressing sensitivities to another's views.

Communication initiates connection and growth. It is the most important process in human existence. Words have a powerful energy to shape thinking, imaging, and feelings. In fact, words make

DAY 2

people. Essentially, positive words make positive people. Negative words make negative people. If you want to change your life for the better, change your words to yourself and others.

When people communicate with you, the goal is shared meaning, understanding and prompting some action or behavioral response. What kind of energy comes with that kind of communication? It is a very positive energy that tends to draw people to you. It implies openness, flexibility, interest in others and understanding various viewpoints. Communication generates a much more positive energy and approach.

Building rapport with people is an important skill in business. Seeking to understand customer needs requires proficiency in two skills, good questioning techniques and listening to learn. Would you give your business to someone who is approaching you from domination and isolation? Probably not. Would you give your business to someone who is seeking to communicate, be open, ask questions, listen carefully, and respond appropriately toward your best interests?

Experiences in Spirit

Zayd's notes: "I became aware that communicating openly is easier said than done. I have a tendency to talk more than I listen. In my first conversation of the day, I talked closer to 80% of the time and was unaware until afterwards. In a later conversation with my wife, I was aware and allowed myself to listen more and talk less. As I listened I saw the value of her viewpoints, even though they were different than mine. By listening for shared understanding, it seemed easy to come to agreement on the central issue needing attention. There was no tension. I felt patient, calm, and peaceful."

One research participant reported: "My tendency has been to try to solve the problem. After reading the 2nd day, I called my sister back because I felt that I didn't listen adequately. My reflections were: 'I wondered if I communicated with her openly.' I said: 'No, I didn't. I did most of the talking.' I called her back. This time I listened. I felt better. There was a difference because I wasn't trying to solve the problem; just listening and only responding."

"This exercise helped me understand that listening is not trying to give a person the answer, but responding when asked to respond. I'm not planning this stuff. It's a law of attraction. Once you put your focus on certain words and images, then the law of attraction kicks in."

DAY 2

Actions for Today:

1. Write the affirmation 15 times

   I am open communication

2. Show genuine interest in people today by asking open ended questions about their interests and life situations.

3. Listen 80% of the time and talk only 20% of the time in your conversations

4. Reflect on today's lessons and write your thoughts and feelings in your journal.

Today I Am Connecting With People

Isolation or Connection?

All of these contrasting energies come from our experience in this temporary physical life. Ego creates isolation and separation. When one is selfish and dominating they may tend to isolate themselves from people. For example, think of someone you know that you perceive as selfish. Maybe someone you work with who dominates the meetings and is very competitive within the team. What would be your normal response if they were coming towards you in the hallway? Would you run up to them and give them a hug? Or would your natural tendency be to turn away and avoid contact with that person? In many instances it would be avoidance. The energy of isolation has been generated because selfishness and domination led to separation.

Imagine a prisoner who is in solitary confinement, isolated from the general population. In many instances, this isolation occurred because of some ego-based action. Maybe they stabbed someone or fought someone. You could argue that it was for survival and self-defense in that environment. Maybe or maybe not. However, whatever it was, it resulted in separation and isolation. This is a metaphor or image of what ego is ultimately striving to do in its selfishness and domination. It wants to isolate you from others by putting your mind in "solitary confinement."

However, when you consider being selfless and serving others while communicating through the processes of questioning and listening, you establish a connection with people. The connection is more than just a physical connection. In what we perceive as the spiritual world, there is no separation. Everything is connected and not limited by any physical dimension of time, space and/or distance.

DAY 3

Spirit is boundless and the connection is limitless. This is why the words and work of the great messengers, prophets, leaders and teachers throughout history live on. They were models of human excellence. They established connections and are still remembered, talked about often and followed regularly. Even though some of them lived centuries ago, they are still living on in the minds and hearts of people because spirit is limitless. The connection is limitless. The connection occurs because of what has been communicated of words, concepts, feelings, emotions, and images that live on.

Experiences in Spirit

Zayd's notes: "I felt one with spirit today and had wonderful quiet time during the evening. Writing the positive words in a note of connection to a friend was very powerful. The words generated energy as I was writing them and I felt better."

One research participant wrote: "The connection at some level was very clear, but at another level it seemed a bit obscure. My intention in going (to a group study session) was to connect spiritually, but I don't know if at the interpersonal level I achieved that connection. I think what I might need to do to connect with people is to be more still and pay more attention to my surroundings. Where I do think I am connecting it tends to be a very subtle experience where I feel at peace to be listening to someone share something or just by being there with good intentions. There's a connection there, but I find it a little difficult to verbalize what that feels like exactly."

"Where my connecting became really deep and almost tangible is when I sat down to write the connecting note. Oddly enough the day before, I read this assignment to a friend of mine. She told me that she had written a letter to God. That day I made up my mind to write a letter to God, but I hadn't decided yet when I would do that. The next morning when I read this assignment I couldn't help but think that it would be helpful to try that today. I know that I was supposed to connect with people, but I felt like I needed so badly to connect with The Source of Spirit before I could connect with people…"

"Tonight, however, I inadvertently achieved something so ground breaking and I am so glad I wrote this letter to God. It wasn't like writing any normal note. And it was about my connection with Him. I felt very tense while writing the letter, words just poured like a river. I felt like I had let so much out of me and that I had needed to do this for so long. When I got to the bottom of the page I was interrupted, but I had already began to form a sense of relief that I had never felt before. I smiled at the thought that I would never have to leave my seat to deliver this note. It had already been delivered. I know this assignment had a different intent for me, but I am so grateful for it's leading me where it led me. Overall, this experience today has been very enlightening and eye opening. I know that soon I will do a better job in connecting with people."

DAY 3

Actions for Today:

1. Write this affirmation 15 times

   I am connection

2. Be aware that everything is connected spiritually. Look beyond physical differences to see the connections on the spiritual and mental levels

3. Write a handwritten letter to G-d expressing your feelings and thoughts. Or write someone a hand written note to express some feeling of connection with them. Tell them how you feel about them and why you connect with them.

4. Reflect on today's lessons and write down your thoughts and feelings in your journal.

DAY 4

Today I Am Fully Present in Each Moment

Past or Present?

Another contrast is the focus of time. Ego loves to focus on the past and the future. Ego's selfishness, dominance, and isolation turn its view to the way things were in the past. Since the way things were is known to the ego, it wants to create a future that looks like the past. That's why you hear people talk about "the good old days" and wanting to return to them. You see so many references made by people to: "What we did yesterday." "Let me tell you about what I used to do." "The last time we did that such and such happened." "The last time we were together, this is what you did."

Well, what happened in the past doesn't mean that's what will happen in the present. Yet, ego doesn't want to let go of the past. It wants to relive the past. By constantly focusing attention on the past the ego keeps you from manifesting the present. The habits of attitude and patterns of behavior from the past get carried over into the present. Some people's current life situations are seen through lenses of the past. As long as ego can keep you stuck there, then it's doing its job of protecting its own selfish environment. It does not want to allow you to move beyond what it has generated and wanted from the past.

Remember G-d created humanity. Overtime, He fashioned him and breathed into him from His Spirit. He made for you the abilities to hear, listen, pay attention and learn. He made for you the faculty of sight and vision. And He made for you feeling in the heart.

There is One Spirit of life which is G-d's breathe into humans. The human being has a spirit which is defined as soul, psyche, mind,

DAY 4

self or personality. There is a big difference between G-d's spirit and the human soul.

The word "ego" in this writing refers to the diseased ego based in fear, doubt, worry, and selfishness. The natural healthy ego is good. A healthy sense of "I" as part of the whole of creation. The "I" which accepts its responsibility to contribute its service to the whole of creation. Yet, the ego can become diseased when it discounts the whole and sees itself as the center of every situation. The selfish I, I, I and me, me, me. This selfishness causes problems for individuals and the whole. Ego's desire takes things out of balance and limits the outcomes.

Some people live their lives wondering why they can't move forward and get to a different future. It's because they are stuck in the past. Pay attention to people's conversations at work and in the family. Listen to how many references are made to the past. Listen to yourself in your conversations. Listen to how you talk and recognize that when frequent references are made about the past, that's your diseased ego speaking and keeping you stuck.

The past is not totally irrelevant. Of course, you can learn from the past, if you choose to. There are many lessons that have occurred in the past. Whatever the lesson was from the past can be applied in the present. However, learning from the past is not the same as being stuck in the past. Every time you flash back to the past in your thoughts, words, images, and emotions, then you are in fact living in the past, in that moment.

The problem is when your fears surface because of past thoughts, images, and feelings. It's interesting because maybe something happened 20 or 30 years. The ego will bring that past incident up as if it happened yesterday; as if it happened an hour ago, a minute ago. In fact, it will make you relive it as if it's happening in the present because of delusions and illusions. The ego tricks you into thinking "I've got to maintain the same habit because that's what I did in the past." When that's really not true; you always have a choice. Is that true? Do you always have to do what you did in the past? Or do you have a choice?

DAY 4

Spirit is calling you to express that choice of being in the present moment and focus on what's happening now. That's the only time that is real anyway. The past is over. It can't be relived. You can't bring it back; except ego brings it back in your mind. If the result was negative the ego becomes afraid that what happened in the past will happen again. The future is not here yet. So it can't be changed.

We say contrasting energy and points of attraction because by focusing on the past the ego invites the past to show up again in the present. Then it becomes a revolving door of experiences that's never ending. This is why you see patterns repeated again and again and again. You get to a certain point and that ego perspective kicks in. Then you seem to be reliving something that occurred previously. Even though now your body is different; your mind is at a different stage of development; you're different in the physical life; yet, that same circumstance seems to be relived again.

In fear ego keeps you stuck. FEAR can be defined as False Evidence Appearing Real. There are two aspects to whatever we fear. First, it's not real. It doesn't exist in the moment. Second, it's future oriented, meaning it hasn't happened yet. How silly is it to be afraid of something that's not real and hasn't even happened yet? Yet, we do have fear sometimes.

Ego is trying to keep you trapped in past perspectives. The world of spirit is moving forward; it's evolving. Look at the generational differences. Look at what's happening in technology. Look at what's happening in the evolution of thought regarding spirituality. Look at what's happening in business; in all the fields of education, business, economics and government. Can you see how things are constantly evolving and expanding? But, ego still wants to go back to the past. It wants to relive the past. "If I could just have it the way it used to be, then everything would be fine." No, it won't be fine by going backwards because now is not like it used to be.

DAY 4

Now is now! In a moment, a few seconds, this now moment will become the past. The new moment will be the present. And the next moment will be the future. The only way you can get whatever future you want is by focusing, being, living and energizing in the present moment with what feels good and is rationally intelligent. Focus on what feels like the appropriate action toward the good in this moment. Spirit is what cultivates that perspective.

Being present in the moment is about awareness. This is the real gift in life. Awareness! Consciousness of what is "now" in this moment. This means allowing your mind to block out thoughts of the past or future in order to be aware in the moment. This type of focus requires concentration. A focus on the present gives concentration to the task at hand. That concentration improves one's ability to enhance the quality of any experience. Colors are more vivid and alive. Sounds are clearer. Everything seems more intense and alive when we live in the present moment. Dr. Spencer Johnson wrote a book titled *"The Precious Present."* The point of the story is this present moment is a gift to be used. That's why it's called The Present.

Experiences in Spirit

Zayd's notes: "Today is my birthday. What a magnificent day! Extremely high energy all day. I was able to slow down at moments to concentrate on being aware in the present. The focus on portions of conversations was more intense. Food tasted a little different. I became aware that the pattern of eating and chewing fast is a habit. Awareness in the present requires one to break that habit. Creating a new habit will take time as it is a process. However, continuing to practice would lead to richer experiences."

One research participant stated: "I am living with someone with a huge ego. I can't go against her ego. If I do, she tries to win at all costs. In the past, my response to people with big egos was to go "toe-to-toe." 'Oh, you want to fight, then let's get it on.' Now, I am not going there with her. I'm not putting my energy into ego that way. I'm not wanting to get revenge. The ego part wants to get revenge; to take her to court. The concepts have really helped me to stay more in spirit, through this whole ordeal. It helps me digest the situation. What do I do when ego wants to take control of me? Now I have knowledge and can articulate what to do – in spirit."

Another participant wrote: "Another significant behavioral change occurred after working with 'being present.' During a late summer evening, I was dining alone outside of a restaurant in Washington, DC. Generally, I would have rushed through the meal and rushed back to my room to work. Instead, I chose to really be present."

"It was pleasant to sit quietly and observe. People were laughing and talking and the wait staff was particularly attentive. If a wine glass was empty, they filled it. If a dish was empty, they unobtrusively removed clutter. Every time the staff came to my table, I calmly looked them in the eyes and thanked them. It was truly a blissful experience. I even ordered dessert – it was luscious!"

"My phone rang at the end of the meal and instinctively I answered it just as the waitperson arrived to give me the bill. I quietly said to the person that I would call them back. As the waitperson handed me the bill, he quietly said, 'Your dessert was on the house. We all enjoyed you dining with us this evening.' I was totally blown away! Not so much about receiving something for free. It was about receiving the gift of being present with people who wanted and deserved to be noticed and they truly appreciated it. This particular behavior is something that I am working with, and journaling with, because I have found that the most pleasant part of being present is that the company is always great – even if the company is myself."

DAY 4

Actions for Today:

1. Write this affirmation 15 times

   I am awareness in the present moment

2. Do one thing at a time today. Concentrate intensely; rather, put all of your attention on each task you are working on in any given moment. When reading, concentrate entirely on reading. When eating, concentrate entirely on eating. Just for today, no reading while you are eating. Slow down and pay attention to every bite, every chew; every taste; and every swallow. Fully embrace all aspects of the eating experience. When communicating with someone, put all of your attention on them in the present moment.

3. Reflect on today's lessons and write down your thoughts and feelings in your journal.

DAY 5

Today I Am Being More
Fully Who I Am

Doing or Being?

Ego is all about doing. Spirit is all about being. Yes, in this journey there is action; there are things to be done. No doubt! But ego tricks us into thinking we are only here to do. And if we're not doing it, then we're not accomplishing. If we're not doing, then something is wrong.

Imagine the days when you have a long "to do" list. Do you feel overwhelmed with how much you have to do? Maybe you have 15 items on that list and only get three things done. How do you feel? Well, some would say I feel good about getting the three things done. Yes, but how do you feel in relation to those other 12? Often people feel a sense of failure that they didn't accomplish all they set out to do for the day. In reality, it's highly unlikely to get 15 things done in a day because there is not enough time, especially in life during the 21st century. However, ego tricks us into this "doing" perspective that 'it's all about what you do.' People tend to talk with each other from this energy of "doing."

Some people define themselves by what they do. When you go to a business networking event and meet someone; what is the first thing they ask you? "What do you do?" They want to know what you do before knowing anything else about you. Yet, another perspective says: What you do seems to be secondary to what and who you are. Don't you do what you do because of who you are? Then, who and what are you?

Being is much more powerful than doing. I can't explain it fully. You have to experience it for yourself. However, which comes first doing or being? Can you do something before you are being it? Well,

DAY 5

we could have a good debate about that. The point here is that ego focuses mostly on doing. You do this one thing or you don't do it. Sometimes that can become a limitation and a habit. When you allow yourself to be, then alternatives may show up to give you better options than the one thing you decided to do.

On the other side, spirit focuses energy less on doing and more on being. I often say: "life is more about being who you are, what you are, and where you are supposed to be." Thereafter, the energies of spirit will take over through communication, connection and being in the present moment. Then what's for you will be drawn to you through the world of spirit. What's for you will not pass you by. What passes you by was not for you. We can't explain, in a rational way, how "things" show up, because things of spirit are not rational. Again, our knowledge is too limited to fully comprehend spirit. Yet, our experience teaches us the truth of expansion through being and aligning with spiritual power.

For example, you have a thought in your mind. You create an image to match that thought. You have an emotion to match the image and then you leave it alone. Thereafter, in a certain season or period of time, the thoughts and feelings manifest physically. Some things manifest within minutes, hours, days, weeks, months and/or even years. That's how spirit is. That's how the connection is. That's how being is. Once you focus on being, you don't worry about what you have to do or what's being done. Doing seems to take care of itself. It becomes secondary and less relevant. It seems that what needs to be done will show up to match your being.

Being is what's most important. Think about the other creatures living on this earth. Certainly they have tasks, things to do. They have families and communities just like human beings. The giraffe out in the forest -– is it doing or being? The lion in the plains -- is it doing or being? Yes, they are doing something when they get hungry. When they go to look for food, they are doing something. When they are protecting themselves, they are doing somethings. Outside of that how do these creatures spend most of their time? Being or doing? These creatures are being true to the nature and characteristics of what they are: lions and giraffes.

With the human being, it's diseased ego has it reversed. The ego wants you to spend more of your time doing and not being. It can create a physical, mental and emotional imbalance. Some people work 20 hours a day because of a perception of "I've got to do; got to get this done." The pressure of extreme doing over time can create stress and illness. Think about it: Are we human doings? Or are we human beings? So what is our essence? Our essence is being. Our essence is being what we are with the nature and characteristics of humanness and spiritness. Being what you are goes far beyond this physical journey.

What is your essence? Is it physical? The physical capabilities will change throughout the aging process. One could loose a physical limb, but does that make them less human? Physical cannot be the essence. What about your mental capabilities? Is that the essence of you? Would you be any less human if you had a mental illness or diminished mental capacity? Mental cannot be the essence.

What is your essence? We ask you to consider this answer: Your essence is spiritual! You are a spiritual being in a physical body. When that body expires, the essence of you – spirit will move on too. Where it goes, I don't know. It came from somewhere before entering the physical body. I believe spirit lives on beyond the physical body. You are encouraged to live with this perspective just for today. Try it on and see what happens; see how you like it.

Experiences in Spirit

Zayd's notes: "As I start the day I observed myself having some discomfort "trying" on this idea of being. I know it's true – I am

DAY 5

a spiritual being. However, this view really challenges patterns of conditioning. Where else have I given this much time to focus on being? How many people are aware of this perspective? As I observe myself driving in rush hour traffic, I wonder or think maybe very few of the hundreds of people around me are aware of their "being ness" in this moment. So much energy is placed on doing the driving; what has to be <u>done</u> at work; and/or what was done yesterday. I am observing myself being in the hustle and bustle. Cars speeding, everyone seems to be in a hurry to get where they are going. I pulled off the road, onto a parking lot and experienced less hustle and bustle."

"Yesterday's focus has transferred over into today. I find myself slowing down eating and being more present in the moment. For example, I used my tongue to feel the texture of the food change as a result of chewing. Thereby, noticing the difference in the texture of a tomato and a piece of lettuce. Each type of food has its own nature, characteristics and attributes. Some food are high in potassium, while others are high in sodium. Each type of food is uniquely designed, shaped and engineered for a purpose. I observed the food go down my throat as I swallowed. What a wonderful, marvelous process that has been engineered by the Creator. The ability to chew, break the food down into a texture that can be swallowed and eventually digested more easily."

One participant wrote: "The praise is to God, I am having great experiences AND things are getting a whole lot better. Glory to God, <u>being</u> really works. It's very powerful. I didn't even have to do anything." ☺

Actions for Today:

1. Write the affirmation 15 times:

    I am a magnificent being

2. Sit quietly and relax by taking deep slow breaths. Be consciously aware of your inner self looking outwardly through your eyes. Sense that the essence of you, your spirit, is being the observer of you and your surroundings.

3. During the day, try to observe yourself as you do things. Be self observant as if you were outside of your body looking at you.

4. Reflect on today's lessons and write down your thoughts and feelings in your journal.

DAY 6

Today I Am at Ease about Everything

Difficulty or Ease?

Ego loves to give us the view that everything is difficult. Throughout the country, I conduct training sessions where people are seeking to adjust their behaviors and live a better life. When a suggestion is offered, some will say "Oh, that's hard! Or that's difficult to do!" Have you ever said or felt like something you wanted or needed to do would be hard? Well, if that's the perspective, then there's going to be a certain energy that goes with it. It's going to be a point of attraction. Then it will, in fact, be hard and difficult. Why? Because ego has convinced you that it's hard; that it's so difficult. As a result you attract more difficulty to you. But it's a delusion. Things aren't necessarily difficult. It is what it is. Once you can accept that it is what it is, then difficulty is removed. You just follow the logical process to its conclusion.

In fact, from a spiritual perspective things are designed for ease. We're not created because of difficulty. The Creator didn't create us for difficulty. We're in this existence for things to be easy for us. Everything in the universe is subjected to us. It's all serving and each other. Is that ease or difficulty? It only becomes difficult when we resist what is.

Ego loves to resist and "paint" a picture of difficulty. No pain! No gain! If things become difficult long enough, then ego puts us in a perspective of feeling powerless. People begin to think: "Things are so difficult I don't have any power to change it or make it what I want it to be." However, when you are accepting what is; appreciating situations as they are; things become easier because you won't feel the need to "fix" it or come up with the "ideal" solution. Finding the "perfect" solution is stressful. What is the perfect solution? How do we figure out the "best" solution? Circumstances are constantly changing. In some situations, what's perfect today may not be perfect tomorrow.

Instead, life becomes easier when you allow yourself to be present in a situation and not feel like you have to take action or do something. Just focusing on being brings about ease. In reality, life is ease! Once you understand how it works, your life becomes easier. The Source does not want difficulty for you. The Source wants ease for you. Think and feel the experiences of your life that have been filled with mercy after mercy; grace after grace; moment by moment by moment. This has been occurring from the "beginning" to the "end."

Everything in this physical creation is here to serve you. The food serves you with nutrients that support life and growth. Wood, metal, and other elements serve you for shelter, transportation, and protection. Stars serve you for guidance and finding your path. The moon serves you to keep track of time. Non-physical elements serve you as support and guidance. The only difficulty enters your life when you invite it through disobedience to the natural, easy way designed for you by the Creator.

For 40 days, a colleague and I were studying the book "Ask and It is Given" by Jerry and Esther Hicks. We would read 20-25 pages multiple times during the week and discuss them. There were many experiences that happened which we considered evidence of the book's content. Reflection upon the experiences and lessons learned led me to relax more and be present to express joy more often on my journey. The key was the awareness that life is ease.

I began to learn to relax and take life easier because of the awareness that my thoughts and emotions created vibrations to attract into my physical experience whatever I put my attention on. Negative thoughts and feelings attracted more negativity, internally and externally. Positive thoughts and emotions attracted more

DAY 6

positive experiences, internally and externally. The same works for you!

By deciding what you want and aligning your thoughts, emotions, and actions with your intended desire, then it's easy to relax and be at ease with the awareness that what you want is already coming into your experience. The Source of all is bringing to you what you've asked for. By relaxing, you create space to draw unto yourself what you've put your attention on. When relaxed and something doesn't show up or what you thought you wanted moves away from you, then you are at ease because you know that something better is on its way.

For example, you could apply for a job; interview and then be told it was not the best "fit" for the company. Instead of feeling rejection (negative emotion) you focus your awareness on the possibility that this happened for the best reason. That job wasn't for you because something better is for you that will help you be, do, and have more of what you really want. This perspective makes life so easy. All you need to do is clarify what you want and ask for it. Source and the forces in the universe will do the rest. Ask. Trust. Relax. Take it easy and then respond appropriately to what shows up in your experience. Life is ease!

Experiences in Spirit

Zayd's notes: "There is a natural flow. Everything goes better with relaxation and ease. Today may have been the most powerful so far. I'm not sure if that is because of today's focus on ease or an accumulation of the energies of the other days. Each day has naturally led to ease. By being in this energy, it seems that everything is happening right on time."

"Interestingly, there were three incidents today of this. First, when I went into the cleaners there was no line. I was waited on right away. Second, when I went into the post office, there was no line. How often do you go in the post office and not have to wait in line? It's usually a rare occurrence. Third, this focus on relaxing and ease allowed me to slow down and focus on my breathing while walking, sitting, and in all activities. While returning to the car, walking slowing, I was aware of the swaying of the trees in the breeze; the fluttering of the American flag; and a connection with another soul who was driving his car out of the parking lot. It was a special moment. It is a marvelous and easy day; a different, more unique walk today. Very pleasant, relaxed, easy and everything was right on time."

One participant stated: "I'm using the affirmations as a chant to recite the positive affirmations. I live in a basement apartment. When we had the rain storms my living area was flooded. All of my belongings and important student papers were damaged. When I saw this situation, I found myself chanting 'everything is easy; everything is easy' over and over again. Chanting these words changed my mood. It lifted the depression and made me feel functional in the eye of the storm."

Another participant reported: "I called a friend of mine. She's a single parent and going through a lot of stuff. I got a message from her. This chapter gave me the giggles. I was laughing and so relaxed today. When I called her, I had put myself in such a relaxed and easy state. She called me with problems. So I called her back to make sure she was alright."

"When I called her, I'd been in such a relaxed, easy state. My response to her on the phone was: 'I just stopped to ask her how she was doing.' I was so relaxed until she started laughing. She said to me: 'I'd called because I was in such a bad state of mind.' She said my call "made her day." She said she needed to relax; "You seem to be in such a relaxed state. Glad you called me in that state because I needed that. I was feeling intense about going for the new job."

Another participant wrote: "Today I found myself repeating this affirmation during a lot of my time. By the end of the day, I realized

DAY 6

how much of an anxious person I have been. Making myself relax proved to be more challenging than I expected it to be. Each time I felt my ego get up, I sat it down by relaxing my mind and thinking easy. I also used this affirmation to control the endless rush of fears that I have been having. It helped me to instantly relieve some of this tension and stress."

Yet, another participant wrote: "Life being hectic I chose to allow my subconscious to randomly connect with the different responses from spirit. Once "easy" resonated for me, I found a strong inclination to work with the behavior for at least 5 days. Creating a habit for me takes some repetition.

"Ease" showed up for me first. After the first day, I realized that being in "ease" was most significant and so I started my 25-day journey. I catch myself now realizing how much dis-ease I can put out there. People are commenting on how comfortable I am to be around. I've been described as many things, but not generally "easy." My energy level can be quite high and had in the past cost me great effort. Taking time to be – just be is wonderfully relaxing."

Actions for Today:

1. Write this affirmation 15 times

   I am relaxed and at ease about everything

2. Start the morning by sitting comfortably and breathing deeply. As you breathe deeply and slowly, allow every part of your body to relax. Enjoy the feeling of relaxing in the moment.

3. Walk a little slower today. Make it a point to slow down. Avoid rushing around by planning to arrive at your appointment earlier. Give yourself enough time in everything you do today to allow you to relax into it without the need to rush.

4. Reflect on today's lessons and write your thoughts and feelings in your journal.

DAY 7

Today I Am Hopeful

Powerless or Hopeful?

Again ego tricks the human being into a false sense of powerlessness. When one is isolated as opposed to being connected; selfish and not serving others; taking action when they could just be; then they begin to perceive things as difficult. Powerlessness goes along with all of those things. However, consider this: In truth, are you powerless? Or is that perception created by the diseased ego to keep you stuck?

Consider how many people are unhappy in their jobs? Sixty-seven percent of employees are disengaged at work. Is it possible their soul is calling them to evolve to higher levels? Many people are unhappy and know they have potential to be and do more. Yet, they won't move on because of feeling powerless. They won't follow and trust the inspiration of their soul, the message of the inner voice. They may remain because they don't think they have enough power to change themselves or their circumstances.

Whereas the opposite vibration is being hopeful that things can change. Why? In truth, everything will change. Nothing stays the same, except G-d's way of being and doing. From a spiritual perspective, one positive thought and emotion can create hopefulness and begin to change the situation. Just focusing one's attention on being hopeful; the possibility that things can be different automatically shifts the energy and moves one to a new point of attraction. This attracts more possibilities and hope.

To lose hope is the worst of all. Jesse Jackson became famous for his saying: "keep hope alive." Yes, because this is the beginning of moving into even higher levels of positive energy and spirit. When we arrive at hopefulness we begin to accelerate the attraction process.

Experiences in Spirit

Zayd's notes: "Today, I was faced with a potential criticism from students. It came from a third party and no details were given. Ego was hooked. I wanted to respond from ego. It felt very negative. I decided to focus attention on being hopeful that the situation will work out. I felt a need to accept it."

DAY 7

Actions for Today:

1. Write this affirmation 15 times

    I am hopeful

2. Write a list of situations in your life you'd like to change. For each item, write a column of new possibilities and images of what they look like. In the next column write the word: feelings. <u>Write out the positive feelings you associate with the new possibilities and images</u>. In the third column write the words: one positive action I can take today. Write your own chart similar to the one below. Fill in all three columns. Thereafter, TAKE THE ACTION!!!

Possibilities and Images of What They Look Like	Feelings	One Positive Action I Can Take Today

3. Reflect on today's lessons and write your thoughts and feelings in your journal.

4. Review your journal entries for the last week.

DAY 8

Today I Am Responsible For My Life Situations

Victim or Responsible?

As a result of feeling powerless then a person may feel like a victim. "Oh, you did that to me." "It's your fault." "I'm just a victim here, I don't have any responsibility." "Look at what you did to me." "You keep doing that to me." This is a diseased ego. What does the victim attract, except more experiences to feel victimized? Then they'll say: "See I told you this always happens to me. I'm always a victim." Well of course, because that's what they're sending out and attracting.

It's important to make a distinction between being victimized and perceiving oneself as a victim. When tragic things happen to people they may have been victimized. For example, if a woman is a victim of domestic violence, then she has been victimized. It's not her fault. However, as a result of that experience she may begin to perceive herself as a victim. If she makes that choice, then her fear may project that energy into other relationships. Could she feel unworthy and subconsciously expect that type of action? I don't know. I'm just asking. Now, the question is: Because she was victimized, does that mean she should choose to see herself as a victim? No! She doesn't have to see herself as a victim, right? She can't change what happened. It may have been out of her control. But, she can decide to take responsibility for what happens next.

This can apply to social/cultural groups as well. Look at the Black Lives Matters Movement. Some African Americans may have been victimized, but that doesn't mean they have to see themselves as victims, as a group of people. Muslim Americans may be victimized by bigotry during this ISIS phase in history. But, that does not mean they have to see themselves as victims. Lastly, we're experiencing terrorism in the world. Some of these crimes have been committed by Americans against Americans (policemen against "blacks" and the backlash against Muslim Americans) and some by Middle Easterners against the world. Yet, does America, France and allies see themselves as victims or are they taking responsibility for what happens next?

Spirit is saying: "You are not a victim! Take responsibility! Be responsible for everything in your life situations. That doesn't mean you can make everything be what you want; but take responsibility." Within the word responsibility are two words: respond and ability. Taking responsibility means you are willing to respond with your ability. Sometimes you have to take action. Sometimes you respond by just being there. You don't have to do anything but be there and focus your thoughts, images, emotions and energy on the positive. That's a response to the situation too. Maybe no words are spoken, but it can shift the energy. It can shift you out of victim mentality, victim emotion into greater possibilities of response and creativity.

What is the relationship between responsibility and creativity and power? Think for a moment about some organization or company that you know very well. What position has the most responsibility for the success of that company? Most would say the CEO or the top position. What position has the least responsibility for the success of that company? In other words, that position would not be called by television stations and newspapers to answer for the failure of the company. Most people would say a position like the mail sorter or cafeteria server. Of course, those positions are honorable and have important responsibilities. If the mail is not sorted properly then the business cannot be done on time. We need the cafeteria servers to be clean to avoid diseases. However, the mail sorter and cafeteria

DAY 8

server do not have to answer to the Board of Directors for overall company success.

Secondly, think of the concept of power within that organization. Wouldn't the same CEO or top position have the most power within that organization? Likewise, wouldn't the other positions have the least power within the organization? Yes. Why is this important? Because there is a 100% correlation between the amounts of responsibility a person is willing to take on and the amount of power that person will have. So, if you're willing to take full responsibility for everything in your life situations, then you will have more power. I'm defining power as energy and influence.

Lastly, by having more power and influence you will have more opportunity to express human creativity. When you are exercising your creativity, then you are powerful. You are using the power to make something new or reforming it to fulfill your vision and solve everyday life problems that may be blocking your progress. Therefore, the key to moving your life toward more creativity is taking responsibility. What are your abilities? Identify the abilities G-d has given you as a human being? Then, by using your energy to respond creatively to your life situations, you will feel the power you already possess within.

Experiences in Spirit

Zayd's notes: "There seems to be a connection between hopeful and responsible. As I am hopeful about new possibilities for life and resolution of conflict. Hopefulness requires I take responsibility for my attitudes, behaviors, and habits. No way for hope to manifest physically unless there is responsibility. Responsibility then becomes like a bridge to be crossed, to carry one from hopeful to physical manifestation of what is hoped for. It seems that part of taking responsibility is being responsible to stay in spirit."

DAY 8

One person stated: "I am more at peace in the midst of turmoil. There continues to be major life challenges, but I feel like I'm dealing with them in a totally different way. I'm dealing with them in a more spiritual way. Not focusing on why is this happening to me; why am I a victim? Not focusing on that helps me deal with it better."

DAY 8

Actions for Today:

1. Write this affirmation 15 times

   I am responsible.

2. Take at least 30 minutes to do something creative today. Write a song, a poem, a story, a plan; draw a picture; paint a painting; knit or crochet a hat. Use whatever talent for creativity you possess and do something with it today. Be aware of how your feel while doing that creative thing.

3. Reflect on today's lessons and write your thoughts and feelings in your journal.

Today I Am Flexible

Rigid or Flexible?

Sometimes ego can project a rigid view. It sounds like this: "Things have to be this way or something is wrong with it." "You've got to set it up exactly like this." "You've got to say it exactly this way." "It's got to have a certain look." Well, why? Are there no other possibilities? When one becomes rigid, the ego focuses on one possibility which of course is its own view. Being rigid cuts one off from all other infinite possibilities that may be available.

Being flexible implies there are other options. Flexibility and openness invite creativity. Things are ok the way they are. You can be flexible with what is. You can take the viewpoint there is no need to be rigid. Spirit will bring you a possibility that may be much better than the rigid one you hold in mind.

When you trust, then spirit actually brings you the best possibility for you at that time. Because of the spiritual connection everything is moving and flowing in the best way. When we trust and live from the perspective of spirituality, flexibility is inevitable. Whatever comes up, you can say with confidence, "oh, it's fine" because you are flexible.

Experiences in Spirit

Zayd's notes: "Today provided a great opportunity for me to demonstrate flexibility. Very interesting it showed up on the day I was focused on flexible. Maybe things were orchestrated in such a way that I was able to begin to handle the situation because I was focused on flexible. I wonder: Suppose I had been focused in a different direction."

"Well, I began teaching a new graduate class this evening. Some of the students who were judging me from the last class (mentioned in

DAY 9

the experiences during the day of hopeful) are in the new class. Ego was definitely engaged. I felt much negative energy. I was thrown for a "loop" and felt off balance emotionally. I didn't want to deal with them. However, I had a contract to teach the course, so I couldn't run away from the situation although that's what my diseased ego wanted to do. This was the third day I was dealing with the ego energy of feeling judgment."

Action for Today:

1. Write this affirmation 15 times

   I am flexible

2. Take a different route to and/or from work or school today. Show yourself that you are flexible enough to do something differently.

3. During your daily activities, when an opinion or perspective comes up that's different from yours, be flexible and commit to keeping your viewpoint to yourself.

4. Reflect on today's lessons and write your thoughts and feelings in your journal.

DAY 10

Today I Am Content with Everything of My Life

Dissatisfaction or Contentment?

Nothing in life goes exactly the way we want it, all of the time. Have you ever had situations that turned out differently than what you planned or wanted? Did you become dissatisfied with the situation? I've learned that dissatisfaction can be a voice of the ego. It can imply that things are not "right" by the ego's standards. Ego wants to be right at all costs. Consequently, there must be something "wrong" with anything outside of its point of view.

Dissatisfaction implies that things are not perfect the way they are. In other words, ego's dissatisfaction is akin to saying the Creator who directs all matters is making a mistake because ego is dissatisfied with the outcomes. Now, let me ask you a question. Does the Perfect, Infinite, All-Knowing, Most Gracious, Most Merciful, All-Wise power of the universe posses the capability to make a single mistake? I think not.

Ego always wants to be dissatisfied. Nothing's ever right; nothing's ever good enough; there's always something wrong. This type of dissatisfaction continues to attract more dissatisfaction. This is why you have some people who always seem to be dissatisfied. It seems that nothing you do is enough for them. There are people like that. Have you ever had moments when you've been that type of person who was dissatisfied with what others were doing? If so, I ask you to consider: Is it possible that the dissatisfaction you felt from them was partly the diseased ego reflecting your own dissatisfaction with yourself onto that person?

Is it possible that one can project their feelings and thoughts onto someone else? Is it possible that our relationships with others and situations is a direct reflection of our relationship with ourselves? In other words, if one feels insecure about something or someone; could that be a reflection of insecurity as a basic part of their personality that is projected onto the other person? Likewise, when dissatisfaction about someone is expressed; could that reflect one's dissatisfaction with their own self? Ultimately, dissatisfaction keeps one stuck in unproductive behavioral patterns.

Moving up the contrasting energies scale, when you are flexible you open the door for being contentment. Being content means being comfortable with what is; which in a sense is moving up toward acceptance. It is a satisfaction that every situation in life is the way it's supposed to be. The health is what it is. The financial situation is what it is. I'm content with what is, as it is. Contentment is satisfaction. You can be satisfied with what is. Becoming content is as easy as focusing your attention on contentment and satisfaction. If you are dissatisfied, then $1,000,000 will not be enough money for you. You'll want another million and another million. However, if you are content, then whatever you have will be enough and attract more unto you.

Experiences in Spirit

Zayd's notes: "Being content helped me calm down a little about the situation with the students. Last night they questioned some details missing from the syllabus. I was still very uncomfortable. So I decided to go to the scale of contrasting energies and identify which ego energy was consuming me, in the moment. I looked at the ego list and identified my emotional state was at devaluation. I felt devalued and inadequate around these students. It didn't matter, to ego, that for every student dissatisfied with me I could find hundreds of students who were pleased. I was gripped in the ego vice. It was working on me so hard that I began to devalue myself."

DAY 10

"When the ego scale is turned upside down, then the highest of ego is selfish and the lowest is judgment. I had plummeted toward the depths of ego (devaluation) near the bottom third of the scale. Then I remembered that when ego is calling you to one energy, spirit is calling you to the opposite, contrasting energy. Ego's voice is loud, with a lot of noise and motion. Spirit's voice is quiet and soft, sometimes drowned out by the ego noise."

"I decided to focus on appreciation which is the opposite of devaluation. I began to think about what I appreciated about the students' questions and comments. I appreciate and am grateful that they gave me an opportunity to improve, provide more clarity, and to help them learn. To show my appreciation and gratitude I revised the syllabus. By focusing on appreciation I found a solution in spirit and felt good again."

Actions for Today:

1. Write this affirmation 15 times

   I am contentment

2. Write the word "contentment" on a 3X5 card or a slip of paper and carry it around with you today. Keep it someplace (pocket, purse, or calendar) where you will see it many times today. Take it out, look at it, think of one thing you are satisfied with and feel the energy of being content.

3. Just for today, write a list of all things for which you feel satisfaction or contentment.

4. Reflect on today's lessons and write your thoughts and feelings in your journal.

DAY 11

Today I Am Letting Go

Holding Tightly or Letting Go?

Many people have a problem letting things go. Why? Because their ego wants to hold tightly to its rigid view. Not letting go is like when you hold something tight in your fist. For example, make a fist right now. Squeeze your hand and hold it tightly. Go ahead and do it now. Do you feel the tension and pressure? Continue to hold fist tight for at least 15-20 seconds. Is the tension you feel when squeezing your hand natural? Or does it feel more natural to open your hand and let it go?

Make another fist and look at your hand. Do you feel the tension and pressure of squeezing it? When you're holding on tightly, there's no room for anything to get out. Also, there's no room for anything to get in. When you open your hand, release and let things go, you've made space for something else to come into your hand. You've made space to give. This works the same way with your mind. When your mind is closed, nothing can get in. When it's open you can expand your experiences. Ultimately, spirit will bring to you exactly what is best for that time and situation. It may not come instantly, but it will show up at the "right" time and the best way.

Actions for Today:

1. Write this affirmation 15 times

   I am letting things go now

2. Clean out your closet of things that haven't been used in months or years. Let it go!

3. List out those old assumptions about yourself and your life situations that are unproductive for you. Let them go! List the new productive assumptions you want to make a habit. List those positive images and feelings that go along with the new assumptions.

4. Consider anything that's creating stress in your life... Let it go! If it's a relationship gone bad; an old habit; a bad attitude; or anything else that's ego-based; Let it go!

5. Reflect on today's lessons and write your thoughts and feelings in your journal.

DAY 12

Today I Accept Everything As It Is

Control or Acceptance?

If you can let go then you can accept. If you can't let go, then acceptance is not possible. In fact, holding on tightly moves you to control. When a person is responding out of the diseased ego why do they want to control everything? Isn't it because they're not willing to accept something as it is? They haven't let go. They're not content. They're not flexible. Maybe, they're not taking responsibility. Maybe, they're not hopeful they can change. As a result they want to hold on; they want to control the situation. They want to manipulate it. They want to force things in the situation.

In the extreme, control has to do with force; holding on tightly and exercising force to direct things in a certain way. That makes things static or always the same. There's no dynamic-ness in control. It's limiting things to the status quo. That limitation is supported by a concept of attachment. Because you get attached to the result you want to control; which is ultimately ego's perspective of what it sees and wants. Can you be your happiest self from there? Can you really control anyone else besides yourself? Do you sometimes have a challenge controlling yourself? I do sometimes and I'm working on it.

Certainly, everything has meaning within a context. You need to control your budget at work and home. You need to have controls in your business to meet strategic goals. You need to have some self-control in your interactions with others. There are some situations where control makes sense. This type of "good" control might be called discipline which is a slightly different concept. However, what we're talking about is the control that leads to extremes, the ego perspective that limits us; limits you from being what you really want to be.

On the other side of the scale, acceptance means embracing "what is" more fully. It means perceiving the value of yourself and the situation. Acceptance means engaging in the process and energy that is present, in the moment. With acceptance, there is no need to try to influence or control the situation. Acceptance means you trust God; trust yourself; and trust the universal forces enough to respond positively by going with the flow in a loving way. Embracing the moment, the circumstance for whatever it is, without letting additional thoughts and emotions overcome you. This is a trusting acceptance, faith.

Experiences in Spirit

Zayd's notes: "After writing the affirmations, already I feel no need for doing to control or influence anything today. I am developing an attitude of openness for what shows up today; going with the flow – no resistance; full acceptance of whatever."

"I received a call from the university and was asked to take two new students in the class as an emergency, although the semester was at least two weeks old. I accepted the two students. Today, I also accepted every phone call. I accepted an invitation to attend the graduation of a training program, on the next day. I usually don't accept last minute invitations because the schedule is so full. However, since this was the day of acceptance, I accepted it openly with no question. It feels good to accept. It was easy."

"Acceptance opens up possibilities. By accepting to attend the training program graduation a dialogue was opened up a person of influence. First, this person agreed to allow me to be a graduation speaker for the program, in the future. Second, she saw the vision and impact of the concept of this new book and wants to introduce me to friends who have influence with high level celebrities and national/international cable television programs. She also agreed to introduce me to a senior leader within a global consulting firm to discuss a new service my company is rolling out. Whether these things happen or not is secondary. The fact is this day of acceptance seemed to open the "door of possibility."

Actions for Today:

1. Write this affirmation 15 times

   I am acceptance

2. Breathe deeply, relax and say aloud to yourself at least seven times: <u>Your Name</u>, I accept you totally as you are.

3. Just for today remind yourself of the truth that: As you accept yourself, then you will be accepted by everyone else.

4. Accept every comment and/or action that comes your way today. Remind yourself frequently of today's affirmation.

5. Reflect on today's lessons and write your thoughts and feelings in your journal.

DAY 13

Today I Surrender To What Is

Aggression or Surrender?

Aggression is an ego-based energy related to competition and force. An example would be aggressive drivers. Sometimes this turns into road rage. Through aggression and/or anger people put themselves and others in danger. Look at the word d*anger*. Isn't anger at the core of danger? Anger is the essential and greater part of d*anger*. This anger and competition shows up as speeding in and out of traffic, honking the horn, maybe even screaming profanity at others. As if they could hear. The rage of ego showing up in the energy of impatience, frustration and anger creates a negatively charged atmosphere that can often be out of control. For example, damage to cars and people occurs through aggressive driving. Aggressive driving can cause death. Aggression is a concept of <u>force</u>; forcing one's will on the situation.

On the other hand, surrender is a concept of <u>power</u>. It is related to submission. A classic picture of surrender is the white flag raised during war time. This means they have "given up" and "given in" to the situation. They have chosen to do something different than what they were doing. They are saying "I accept the situation as it is. I give in to what is." As a result, they get to live another day. In addition, they accept whatever comes afterwards from the one they surrender to.

In his book, *The Power of Intention*, Dr. Wayne Dyer says surrender is "...when you allow yourself to be carried by the force that turns acorns into oak trees..." It is as easy for the Creator to make the galaxies as He makes a mosquito. He says: "Be! Then it is." When we surrender to His power, we are submitting to what is and what is yet to come. We submit to the power of the One

DAY 13

who cares for all and uses everything to bring about His will. His "tools" are sometimes invisible, unseen, and unheard of, yet they are available to serve you from ways unimaginable to you. When you surrender, life becomes easier because you don't have to do everything. You trust the Source to do it all. Your job becomes improving yourself; being closer to Source; showing up wherever you're supposed to be; and doing the job given to you by the Almighty, The Most High.

Experiences in Spirit

Zayd's notes: "Today, I was aware of surrendering to whatever showed up. It felt a lot like yesterday's acceptance, yet a little different. Surrender is a powerful energy. Feels like I'm being carried along. It's like floating or soaring on the wind. Maybe this is what a bird feels like while gliding on the wind. Through surrender I felt no stress."

"Two amazing things happened today. First, during the early evening I was doing my best to prepare to catch a train from Maryland to New York City at 5:22 pm on Friday evening. When I found myself rushing, I surrendered to the fact that I could not make it to the Amtrak train station on time. It was 4:00 pm and I had at least one hour's drive through rush hour traffic. I called my colleague to say, I'd leave early Saturday morning. Surrender in this situation opened me up to have a wonderful evening with my wife before going out of town for three days. We had a lovely dinner and went to a movie. It was a perfect way for both of us to end a very busy week."

"The second incident occurred at the restaurant. There is a dish with salmon and a variety of vegetables that is served at the P.F. Chaing's restaurant chain. We've eaten at this restaurant several times over the years. Although I've always wanted the vegetables (shitake mushrooms, bok choy, and asparagus) that are served with the salmon, I've never ordered the dish because they undercook the salmon for my tastes. It's served almost like sushi. I like salmon "well done." They just don't serve it that way and the chef wouldn't cook it well done. Or at least that's what I was told. Therefore, I ordered the meal with sea bass and spinach. I've ordered the same thing every time we've eaten there."

"I ordered the sea bass again. Yet, when it came there was no spinach. The fish sat on top of mixed vegetables. It looked so different than what I've ordered in the past, I thought it was a different dish. I questioned in my mind and with my wife momentarily, then I remembered today was a day of surrender. So I surrendered to the dish as it was and began to put spoonful's on my plate."

"The amazing thing is that the veggies under the fish were shitake mushrooms, bok choy, asparagus, baby corn and red peppers. I was blown away! These were exactly the veggies I wanted! Not only had I wanted them tonight, I had wanted them for years. Why was it different tonight? Earlier that day, there was a spinach alert announced in the news. There was bad spinach circulating in the marketplace. Several people became seriously ill with ecoli and at least one person died. Consequently, on this day, the restaurant threw away all of their spinach and served that dish with those replacement veggies. There were other veggies available, but they chose those veggies for the dish."

"Do you think it was a coincidence? Through surrender, spirit delivered again. It was the best meal I've ever eaten at the restaurant. I told the manager how good it was. He said 'they may want to consider changing the menu to serve the sea bass with those veggies.' It was just that good. Amazing! Absolutely amazing!"

"What is the deeper meaning of these two incident? First, when surrendering to what is, there is no need to rush or to hurry. When taking things as they are, in their own time, then moment by moment will be perfect and easy. Second, through surrender you will get exactly what you want and it will be better than anything you've experienced before."

DAY 13

Actions for Today:

1. Write this affirmation 15 times.

   I am surrender

2. Allow yourself to be aware and submit to the events that show up today.

3. Look for the deeper meaning of your experiences. What are the specific lessons?

4. Reflect on today's lessons and write your thoughts and feelings in your journal.

Today I Am Detached From Specific Results

Attachment or Detachment?

The ego can be rigid, controlling, ad attached to an outcome that may or may not show up. This attachment creates and attracts negative energy. Many people are so attached to outcomes that if it is what they want, then they are overcome with high positive emotion. On the other hand, when things are not as they want them to be, then they are overcome with lower negative emotions. Their emotional life is like a roller coaster ride; high peaks and low valleys of emotions. This could be described as emotional imbalance.

Spirit focuses on detachment. Detachment is living one's life on a steady emotional plane that doesn't spike. Whatever happens can be perceived as good or bad. Detachment says accept it without the emotional swings. This allows one to maintain a balance.

Flexibility and hope raise our consciousness because of the connections; being in the present; being responsible; flexible; content; letting things go; and accepting "what is." Then it's easy to surrender to the situation and detach one's self from the outcomes. Detachment means doing your best effort and maintaining calmness about whatever outcomes manifest. Detachment is when you are emotionally neutral. You become so removed from the outcome that you don't feel an emotion swing one way or the other. Not too high and not too low. Detachment knows that the best outcome will show up at the right time.

Think about it, does the outcome really belong to you? If your ideas are not accepted by someone else, does it really matter? If your performance appraisal is not as high as you want it to be, will

DAY 14

your world come to an end? You show up, do your best and have no worry about the outcomes. Detachment is being void of worry. There's no need for attachment in any dimension. When we can detach, then it's easier to appreciate.

Actions for Today:

1. Write this affirmation 15 times

   I am detached from all outcomes

2. Just for today, allow yourself to step back from outcomes. See them as things that happen as they are supposed to. Recognize there is a higher plan for your life. All outcomes are being orchestrated through spiritual forces that are infinitely intelligent.

3. Remind yourself throughout the day that "it is what it is" and "everything is as it should be."

4. Reflect on today's lessons and write your thoughts and feelings in your journal.

5. Review your journal entries for the last week.

DAY 15

Today I Am Appreciating Everything of My Life

Devaluation or Appreciation?

E go always wants to devalue everything. "It's not good enough." "It's not valuable enough." It makes you think you're not valuable. Ego doesn't perceive itself as valuable. Therefore, underlying statements within one's self-dialogue might be "I'm not valuable. I'm not good enough." This is diseased ego talk that may stem from decades of negative conditioning. When you were a child there was much negative conditioning from parents, teachers, friends, and social/cultural messages. Have you ever heard others tell you OR even worse told yourself phrases like: "Don't do this." "Don't do that." "I can't do such and such?" These types of messages cause insecurity and create a false perception about your true self.

Insecurities stem from ego's devaluation of itself and everything else. It's hard to appreciate anything that you don't value. When one doesn't value themselves, then they tend to not value others and those things manifested in their lives.

Devaluation is built into our view of many commodities. For example, when you buy a new car, it has a price. The more you use it, in fact, as soon as you drive your new car off the lot, it is devalued. Why? Why is it worth less now than it was and it hasn't even been used? It seems to be a concept of ego. The things that are new are valued and appreciated. The things that are "old" are not valued.

Spirit says appreciate everything. Appreciating the old and the new; appreciating the past and the present; appreciating the difference; appreciating the sameness; appreciating the connections. It's easy to value what you appreciate. It's easy to appreciate what you value. Appreciation is a very powerful energy and point of attraction that brings unto you even more things to appreciate.

What would it be like if you decided to live your life appreciating everything that shows up? Recognize that any of these ego perspectives discussed in this book, 9 times out of 10, are your resistances toward the situation. Your resistance is the only thing that's keeping you from moving to where you want to be. Whereas appreciation, gratitude and other positive energies of spirit are moving you toward what you want. When you appreciate, it becomes easier to be patient.

Experiences in Spirit

One participant wrote: "Appreciation feels good. It helped me pay closer attention to my surroundings and the things I'm grateful for. As tired as I feel now that my day is over, I feel so at peace with myself and those around me. It's very comforting."

DAY 15

Actions for Today:

1. Write this affirmation 15 times

   I am appreciation and gratitude

2. Write a list of all things you appreciate about your life and write one word to describe your feelings about what you appreciate. Allow yourself to do that for those areas of your life that are not satisfying in the moment. Remember, those situations are teaching you valuable lessons as long as you allow yourself to learn from them. Appreciate them, feel the positive energy around them, and attract more positives to you.

Things I Appreciate	Feeling About What I Appreciate

3. Reflect on today's lessons and write your thoughts and feelings in your journal.

Today I Am Patience

Frustration or Patience?

Ego wants things to be frustrating. Being impatient, frustrated, and irritable sounds like: "Hurry up!" "Things aren't happening fast enough." Truthfully, things happen when they're supposed to. Just because you planted the "seed" yesterday doesn't mean you'll have fruit on the tree today. That's not how things work. There's a natural order to everything that can be understood which alleviates frustration, over time.

For example, there's a natural process that requires a farmer to be patient. The seed is planted in the earth. Even though he doesn't see it, the seed germinates and goes through a process of sprouting in the earth. In time, the sprout grows and bursts through the earth. It continues to grow until it becomes a tree. Eventually, the tree bears fruit. Initially, the fruit is at an early stage, small and unripe. When it matures, it becomes useful. All of these stages of growth take time. Your life is the same way. Stay in the process of planting seeds and doing the work with perseverance. It is necessary for growth.

Patience is waiting calmly and faithfully for the outcomes to manifest physically. Like the farmer, do your work and be patient. Patience is accepting, appreciating, and waiting without complaint. This quality is very important because people are so impatient sometimes. The ego is impatient. It wants things right NOW! In fact, it wants things yesterday. It wants it from the past. It wants the present in the past and brings the past into the present. Frustration then sets in. Frustration can lead to anger.

Spirit invites you to be patient. It says to you: "It's ok, everything is fine." "Take it easy, its fine." "It'll show up when and how it's supposed to." When you can be patient, then you can be in silence

DAY 16

which leads to stillness. This allows you to continue moving up the awareness scale in positivity.

Experiences in Spirit

Zayd's notes: "Today I found myself a little nervous, anxious about something. I identified my energy at frustration on the chart of contrasting energies/points of attraction. Then I decided to focus my point of attraction on patience. Began repeating the affirmation, silently, I am patient."

"During the morning there was a teleconference meeting with three other persons. I was aware of my perception that the pace of the conversation was slow. The longer people talked the more ego said things like: "This is going so slow. Come on hurry up and finish your point." I was consciously aware of my need to be patient. It's almost as if I attracted this situation that required me to be patient, since I was consciously focusing on patience for today. Another perspective is that my awareness was heightened so I saw the opportunity for patience."

"I worked hard to listen to what people were saying (be in the present moment) and not interrupt them. It was a test to see if I could be patient. What I felt inside was much different than what was projected outside. Inside I was very aware of my feelings and energy to be quiet, listen, and allow people to talk as long as they needed without interrupting. Yet, they did not know what I was thinking and feeling inside. We did accomplish our purpose for the meeting. The client was happy. I felt good that I passed the test of patience in that moment."

One research participant reported: "I'm noticing the way I'm dealing with patience; the divorce and why it's taking so long. People are not responding. I used to ask: Why isn't this happening? Why did that happen? Instead of whining so much, I'm just methodically taking action. For example, I was not happy with my first attorney so I fired him and got another one. By having patience about getting to resolution; I'm getting to the problem solving mode much faster and in a powerful way. I don't feel as victim-like. I feel more in control because I'm operating more in spirit than ego."

Another participant wrote: "Today I realized something huge about myself. I have a problem with my patience. I caught myself behaving and responding impatiently several times. I also noticed that it's not just today that I am not exercising patience like I should. There's a pattern that I am glad I noticed because I can do something about it now."

DAY 16

Actions for Today:

1. Write this affirmation 15 times

   I am patience

2. Identify areas in your life situations (physical, financial, career, family, etc) that are not happening as fast as you like. Be aware of your frustration and impatience. How has that worked for you so far? Now, think of a positive thought and feeling about that situation. Add a statement for whatever lessons that situation is teaching you. Now let it go. Be patient about it. This too shall pass.

Life Situation I'd Like to Improve	Positive Thoughts and Feelings	Deeper Lessons From This Life Situation

3. Reflect on today's lessons and write your thoughts and feelings in your journal.

Today I Am Practicing Silence

Noise or Silence?

Ego loves noise. The louder it is, the better for ego. With noise comes an emotional charge. Imagine a night club like the ones in Hollywood movies. There is so much noise. The music is blasting. People can't hear each other talking, so they must "scream" in order to be heard. People are there to "have fun." They come to a noisy place looking for attention, either from friends or someone they meet.

Many people at night clubs drink alcohol to help them "have fun." I would guess alcohol increases the amount of noise within one's own mind. In some instances, alcohol can lead a person to lose their mind. Many bad things happen when people are drinking alcohol. It seems to impair thinking. Maybe that's why it's not allowed while driving. We know how driving under the influence of alcohol causes tragedy and takes lives. Another sign of its inappropriateness is that alcohol is not allowed at work. When an alcoholic's drinking habit affects their work, they may be fired or at least sent for medical treatment and detoxification. This is not much fun.

The more noise the better for ego. This image of the noise at a nightclub is a metaphor for the noise that ego creates in people's minds. Ego brings many thoughts into the mind one right after another to keep the noise going. Internally, it seems like noise and commotion. It can be so intense that a person may not perceive a way to turn it off. Silence is the way to turn off the noise in your mind and tame the ego.

When there's a lot of noise in an environment, spirit is inviting silence. Silence is an emotional recharging. Just like recharging your battery for your cell phone. Without recharging the battery you will not have enough energy to communicate. Silence helps you recharge your emotional, intellectual, and spiritual batteries. Through silence you increase your awareness of yourself and what is around you. This spiritual perspective can lead you to a new view of your self and the world.

Silence is calmness. Like the calm of a sea or river. Use your imagination to picture a calm sea. Doesn't that picture slow you down? Doesn't it fill you with a sense of calmness? This is what silence can do for you. Keep you calm, increase your awareness, and recharge your battery.

Experiences in Spirit

Zayd's notes: "During a coaching call today I was challenged with keeping silent. I became aware of my tendency to not listen and jump in the conversation. I see that is a pattern I want to break. It is not effective as a coach or a human being. I tried; however, keeping silence was difficult for me. The tendency to talk kept taking over. I learned I need to keep silent and let people finish their statements. I need more practice with silence."

Actions for Today:

1. Write this affirmation 15 times

   I am silence

2. Set aside at least 20 minutes to sit in silence. Turn off the radio and television. Keep your book closed. Sit comfortably upright in a chair with your back straight and your head up. Close your eyes; breathe deeply and be silent. Try your best to turn off your thoughts inside your mind. Try your best to think of nothing. Focus on your breathing. Allow your inner self to be silent too. This may take some days of practice. Be patient with yourself.

3. Practice silence during your meetings and activities, just for today. Strive to listen, be silent and pay attention to your awareness of your self, others, and the environment. Then notice how people respond to your silence.

4. Reflect on today's lessons and write your thoughts and feelings in your journal.

DAY 18

Today I Am Stillness

Motion or Stillness?

Ego loves motion as much as noise. The louder the noise and more vigorous the motion; the better for ego. Some people speak loudly in public. Other have a lot of movement and motion. Sometimes the loud speech and motion is violent and chaotic. They are attracting attention with their noise and motion. That's ego movement through various stages from one extreme to the next – emotional, mental and physical motion. For example, extremely high and low emotional states; working to physical exhaustion due to fear; waking up in the middle of the night worried about some situation. It's one thing to work like that out of love for the work. It's another thing to do it in fear and worry. This can be imbalance created by ego. Yet, spirit is still, so quiet you might not be aware it's there. Yet, it's always there.

Here's an example that creates a mental picture of the contrast between motion and stillness. When a body of water is in motion it's difficult to see *the beauty* underneath. Also, it's difficult to manage the business on the surface. Did you see the movie *Perfect Storm?* There are scenes when the tremendously strong winds on the ocean converged from all angles and created one of the worst storms in history.

The violent motion of the water and wind took over the ship. The crew couldn't stand. Water was washing up onto the boat. The boat was swaying up and down in violent motion. The force of the water was smacking the crew around. They were slipping, falling down, and sliding across the ship's floor. The antenna broke, thereby making the radio inoperable. The force of the water and wind broke the window of the Captain's chambers. All of this chaos made it impossible to stir the ship. No way to get out of the storm. What kind of energy do you have in the moment as you read this paragraph and consider this scene? Do you feel tense?

On the other hand, think of the Caribbean ocean. Like the images on those commercials that say: "It's better in the Bahamas." The blue water is so clear you can see through to the bottom. When the water is still, you can see the wonders that lie "within" the body of water. You see the beautifully colored yellow, blue or grey fish. You see striped fish, spotted fish and fish of all sizes and lengths. The stillness of the clear blue water is peaceful and reveals to you the wonders and treasures within the ocean. How is your energy when considering this peaceful, calm scene of ocean water? Can you feel the difference?

Likewise, it is the same with you. As you learn and allow yourself to be still you will feel calm and serene. As you stay with stillness and look within, you'll discover many treasures that are within you. You'll discover that life has an ease and flow underneath the surface. You'll discover there is a "current" to life that is flowing underneath. That inner flow is connected to spirit. It has a power all its own that may not be seen on the surface. By being still and looking inward you'll open up a new world.

Experiences in Spirit

Zayd's notes: "Stillness is a deeper energy than silence. It's like an extension of silence. Is it possible to be in silence and motion at the same time? Stillness requires motionlessness which supports silence or makes it easier to be in silence. On several occasions today, for a minute or two at a time, I intentionally made myself be still. While in stillness, my awareness of being in silence grew. I was able to be more in silence in a natural and easy way. It felt very calm and peaceful. It seems that stillness supports silence much deeper and is a trigger for peaceful energy."

DAY 18

One participant wrote: "I practiced stillness today and found it to be very soothing. It has a very soothing effect on me. I practiced listening to a speaker for three minutes and focusing just on her. Of course, I had to make a few interjections to let her know I was listening, but this practice was successful. Focusing my energy on her helped me think with more clarity, so eventually when I spoke I had some useful things to say. I also realized that silence even on the phone is meaningful. I used to think that I had to say so much to keep the other party entertained all the time. But when I remained still, it was not awkward at all and the other person continued with what she had in mind. I found it to be helpful for the speaker as well because it allowed her the freedom to speak her mind knowing there wouldn't be an interruption from the other side and more importantly that she is being heard carefully."

Actions for Today:

1. Write this affirmation 15 times

   I am stillness

2. Try this experiment. Focus your attention on someone talking for two minutes. Or if you are alone turn on the radio or television and pay attention to the talking. Notice what you are aware of. Now focus your attention on something in the room that is still for two minutes. Notice what you are aware of. Have you become aware of much more in your environment and within yourself, through your focus on stillness?

3. Allow yourself to sit and be still for 20 minutes a day. Refrain from moving inside and out.

4. Reflect on today's lessons and write your thoughts and feelings in your journal.

DAY 19

Today I Am Peaceful

Conflict or Peace?

Conflict is potentially all around us and within us. Ego works hard to perpetuate these states of conflict. An extreme example of conflict is war. War is the ultimate form of conflict as an ego-based response to human problems. We've seen videotapes of bombings and destruction caused by war in Afghanistan, Iraq, Lebanon, and Israel. We've seen ISIS beheadings and the attacks in Paris. We've seen the devastating toll war takes on human beings who lose loved ones and all of their possessions. Instead of conflict and war, it seems people really want more peace; peace of mind and inner peace.

What is the essence of inner peace? This is a deep question. Peace is not something that is visible in its nature. It is part of the unseen. Certainly, we can see in someone's behavior what appears to be a peaceful attitude; what appears to be relaxed and comfortable. Yet, you may not know what is going on inside of that person's mind. For some who may be introverted in their personality, they may not provide a lot of non-verbal cues in their behavior. Their face or facial expressions may be very bland or neutral or non-expressive. Yet, inside they may be consumed with thoughts, questions, and internal noise. They could be in turmoil inside. However, you would not be able to tell by their facial expressions or non verbal movements that they are concerned. Therefore, a lack of facial expressions may not necessarily indicate peace.

When you ask about inner peace, then you are asking about something that is totally flowing within the individual. Peace is one of the characteristics of the Source. When you focus your attention on spirit and The Source of Peace, then you are left with the power that is beyond your capacity to fully understand.

However, you may catch glimpses of peace in your physical environment. For example, when you see the bird that stands on one foot in the middle of the stream; his leg is so skinny it looks like a stick. As that bird stands so perfectly still, with no movement – you see peace. So there is something about being still inside and outside; about being quiet inside and outside; and being silent inside that has to do with inner peace.

Now there are things outside of you that tend to ignite the peaceful energy. For example, when some people visit a lake or look at the water, they feel peaceful. Others may go to the beach and watch the waves as the tide comes in and feel peaceful. Still others may look at a tree or farmland and feel peaceful. These are outer manifestations of peace. What makes you feel peaceful and relaxed? When we think of the essence of peace, there seems to be something having to do with ease, comfort, stillness, quiet, silence, and security. These seem to be the elements, the boundaries within which one may feel peaceful.

Now, you may ask how does one make, generate, and establish these types of elements within themselves. The only way to find peace is to plug into The Source, The True Owner and Authority in the universe. If you want the energy of peace then there's only One who generates peace. Ultimately, it's peace in the heart, peace in your soul and mind that is the inner peace. This is only comes through the connection with the Source of all Peace.

When you go back and consider those positive qualities around love and joy, appreciation, and the types of energy that comes from those energies of light; then we recognize they have a connection with each other and with peace.

You have an ability to feel glimpses of peace. When you are accepting "what is" in your life situation and moving with your higher self; then you have the freedom to be who and what you are; **the real you**. When your life is moving on purpose, you will experience

DAY 19

peace. When you are performing those activities of remembrance of the Creator; reflecting on the creation and characteristics of Source to generate life and evolve goodness, then you "touch" peace. As long as you are obedient and willing to surrender yourself to what is peaceful and calm in silence and stillness within your own being, then you will experience inner peace.

It's the lower part, the diseased ego, that so many people have given themselves to in complaining, finding fault, blaming, being judgmental and other qualities that remove them from peace. Those energies create conflict. Ego-based energies outlined in the scale of attraction are preceded by questions like: What's in it for me? How do I maintain my selfish viewpoint? How can I dominate the situation? Whose fault is it? Who's to blame? These are just a few such questions of a type of "ego- darkness."

The questions of a type of "spirit-light," lead one towards peace. Questions like: How can I serve? How can we connect? What do I appreciate? What are the lessons from being patient in this situation? How can I respond creatively to the situation with the intent to help? These are just a few questions that lead to the spirit-based energies on the point of attraction scale.

Peace is attainable for you as a human being in how you feel. It's not something you can think of and force through your mental processes. Yes, you can have a thought of being peaceful, but that thought must be aligned with emotions peacefulness, stillness and calmness. Some of that is generated by your knowledge of your connection with Source which is organizing, directing, orchestrating, generating, planning and pulling together everything in a perfect. Source is doing things for you in a way you can't see, hear, feel or even imagine. When you know and experience that as truth, then you begin to understand how everything is connected by Source. The natural result of that perspective is peace.

DAY 19

There's no need for you to do so much to try to generate peace. The need is to BE peace or peaceful. So peace is a state of being more than a state of doing. When you allow yourself to be what you are as a human being connected to Source through your remembrance processes, then you will manifest peace in your attitudes and behaviors. When you are in a peaceful state you will attract more peace to you.

There are so many things in this universe that are at peace and still. When you allow yourself to be aware of the peaceful nature that you possess to be still, quiet, and calm, then that will be the trigger for your energies. Pay attention to thoughts, images, and feelings that help you remain calm, still, peaceful, hopeful, and patient. Peace is very much connected to faith. Your security and peacefulness are because of your faith in Source which connects you with spirit. Through that connection you can be guided along your path to make your contribution in the Light of G-d.

Experiences in Spirit

Zayd's notes: "Today was an easy day. I felt a deeper calm than usual. It went beyond relaxed and easy. Almost felt strange. In the past I was running here and there; worrying about this and that. None of that showed up today. Everything was relaxed, calm, easy, and right on time. I seemed to move about with a knowing, a calm reassurance."

One participant wrote: "After practicing stillness and silence, being calm and peaceful felt really good. The people around me would be flustered up about something and I would find myself smiling in peace. The goal was to observe nature in calm and peace. I have a Japanese Fighter Fish so I decided to spend time observing her. I have had this fish for five months now and I was surprised at the things that I've overlooked since I got her. What I hadn't noticed

DAY 19

is the amount of time she spends in stillness. She can sit for minutes at a time in one corner flapping her tail in peace. I let my eyes rest on her for as long as she sat there. When I dropped her breakfast in her bowl, she made a quick curvy move to snatch the food drops and she chewed hungrily. Her whole body moved in sync with her chewing movements. Then she let her body sway in the water with ease. Watching my fish today reminded me of a song I learned in grade school about how fish live in the sea, they swim all day and feel so free. The hum of this song in my head was very soothing. By the end of my observation I didn't want to go do my work. It felt so good to be calm enough and relaxed like that. So I decided to keep this experience in mind as I moved along throughout today."

Actions for Today:

1. Write this affirmation 15 times

   I am peaceful and calm

2. Allow yourself to be silent, still, and calm as often as possible today.

3. Today spend some time with nature. Visit a lake, a park, a nature trail, etc. Be stillness and silence in nature and experience peacefulness.

4. Reflect on today's lessons and write your thoughts and feelings in your journal.

DAY 20

Today I Am Freedom

Constraint or Freedom?

Ego promotes feelings of being constrained, bound, and limited. A classic example is a person on a job who feels like they can't advance because their supervisor is constraining them. The feeling of constraint continues to attract more things to feel constrained about. Some people may continue to stay in the job and complain about the limitations. Yet, at some point, the employee has become a victim of their own self-imposed limitations. The reality is no limitations exist… except the ones we put on ourselves.

The contrasting energy of constraint is freedom. The person feeling limitations on the job is still free to communicate and negotiate a better relationship with their supervisor. If that does not happen, then they are free to move on to another job in a different organization. However, the ego has tricked them to stay. They would rather remain in a situation that feels bad than exercise their freedom. Why do they stay and feel bad? Isn't it because of fear? Ego has used its force of fear to keep the person from being free.

You are free! If you follow what you've learned so far and free your mind, heart and soul, then you are free to be what you want to be. You are free to do what you want. You are free to have what you want. You have the power and freedom of choice. You can choose to make your life better or not. You can choose responses to your life situations that help you feel good or not. It's your choice! No one can make the choice for you. When you exercise that freedom you are making choices in every moment. By choosing what you want to be and do consistent with your higher self, you will feel better.

You'll find your life will work better through exercising your freedom to choose to live through spirit more often.

Exercising freedom feels much better than constraint. However, please know that freedom is not free. It comes with a price. The price is responsibility. Freedom demands a disciplined response. There is no other way to maintain freedom except through your ability and will to respond in a disciplined manner. Focus, discipline, and hard work will get results in this life. When you make a decision to exercise your freedom you will be challenged to work hard to make that decision "right" for you. Freedom demands that you live up to your potential in human excellence. That is what the spirit energies and points of attraction are all about – EXCELLENCE. Freedom requires you to set goals and take action to achieve them. Take the time to be excellent. Is there any reward for good except good! It is through goal achievement that you will discover your excellence and feel your best!

Experiences in Spirit

Zayd's notes: "Before even reading the lesson, writing the affirmations, and doing the exercise today, I decided not to attend a networking meeting. So often I'd drive for hours to attend meetings because of feeling obligated to attend, not because it was a good strategic decision. Peaceful and calm led me to decide to exercise freedom and not run around to a meeting that is not a priority for my situation now."

DAY 20

Actions for Today:

1. Write this affirmation 15 times

   I am freedom

2. Decide on a goal that you'd like to accomplish today. It must be your goal, not your spouse's, children's, friends', or co-workers' goals. Schedule an appointment with yourself by writing it on your calendar in a time slot. Use that appointment time to accomplish your goal or at least work on it.

3. Reflect on today's lessons and write your thoughts and feelings in your journal.

Today I Am Happiness

Sorrow or Happiness?

After reading this far along in the book, you know that living the positive energies and points of attraction of spirit is a choice. Each day you have chosen to read the pages, write the affirmations, and do the exercises. You have chosen to remind yourself of your daily choices to live in spirit and benefited from the energies that followed.

Sorrow is a choice. Sorrow is like a dark deep hole that is associated with guilt, lose, grief, regret, shame and depression. There is too much sorrow in this world. I choose not to write much about it. I don't like it and have chosen not to put any more energy into it.

Happiness is a choice too. Psychologists say it's not what happens to you that matters, it's your reaction to what happens. You can choose to be happy regardless of whatever shows up in your life situation. If your business is not going as you'd like; you can choose to feel sorrow or choose to be happy. If a relationship is not working out as you planned; you can choose to feel sorrow or be happy. Maybe something better is coming your way. But, it may require a change. Which one will feel better for you, sorrow or happiness? Of course, happiness is the best.

Whatever your life situations are regarding finances, relationships or health, remember they are what they are. It is what it is. It will continue to be what it is until it changes. Since it is what it is, you can choose to be happy while it is or not. Again, it's your choice. Things will continue to be. So why not choose to be happy. The happier you choose to be in the face of your life situations, then the more happiness you will attract to you.

DAY 21

Isn't happiness the major aim of life? Don't you want to be happy? Then why would you give away your happiness to something that is less than you? Why do you give some detail in a life situation the power to make you unhappy? It happened the way it was supposed to. So what! You can still be happy.

You can start being happy by putting a smile on your face. If you practice smiling you will force your self to be happy. Think happy thoughts. Imagine happy images. Feel happy feelings. Be happiness! This is a powerful energy. Once you focus on it your energy will shift to a higher level. So choose to make today a happy day! ☺

Experiences in Spirit

Zayd's notes: "What a wonderful day. I am happy because I can be. I am still here in this physical body. The Source of life has preserved me for another year. I am happy to have another opportunity to get closer to Source; to enhance my relationship with revealed words; to train myself in prayers and to give in charity. My life is wonderful. I am happy. I smiled a lot today."

DAY 21

Actions for Today:

1. Write this affirmation 15 times

   I am happiness

2. Wear a BIG smile on you face. Do it now! That's right smile away right now. Wear that smile all day long and see where it leads you and what it attracts to you.

3. Write a list of all things you are happy about. Consider all areas of your life: spiritual, mental, physical, financial, career, family, and social. Be aware of how you feel after writing this list and throughout the day.

4. Reflect on today's lessons and write your thoughts and feelings in your journal.

5. Review your journal entries for the last week.

DAY 22

Today I Am Joy

Pain or Joy?

A diseased ego promotes emotional and mental pain as a reality. However, it is an illusion. Ego makes up the perception of pain. The more attention one gives it, the more pain one perceives. Yes, physical pain is real. The emotional pain of losing a loved one is real too. Aside from these exceptions, the everyday emotional and mental pain is made up in the mind. The perception that "someone is doing something to you" is a choice. It starts as a choice and continues until it becomes a habit. Consider this question: Are they "doing" something to you OR are you "doing" it to yourself? Is it possible, patterns of negative conditioning have attracted undesirable outcomes?

Have you ever chosen the ego-based pain? I certainly have from time to time. However, you could just as easily choose to see things differently. You could choose to accept the situation. You could choose to appreciate the situation and its lessons. You could choose to take responsibility for your own thoughts, emotions and behaviors. You could choose to leave a "bad" situation and pursue something that feels better. What would be the outcome if any of these choices were made and repeated until they became a habit? You would feel better. There would probably be a more desirable result.

Spirit is calling you to joy. Joy is one of those intangible energies that come and go. Like peace and happiness, it cannot be generated through physical activity. Yet, it is a powerful energy and point of attraction. Joy is a feeling of ecstasy. It is a feeling of lightness and ecstatic happiness. You can be in joy when you focus your attention on joy and being joyful; being content with your situation; and hopeful for better. Yet, it's being hopeful in what is. Joy is accepting what is and having happiness about it. This is joy that comes from Source; a feeling of comfort and happiness.

Joy can be ignited through giving unconditionally. When you give with the pure intention of serving and benefiting others, you will have joy. Giving without wanting anything back in return is a joyful feeling.

Experiences in Spirit

Zayd's notes: "Today was wonderful and easy. It seems that by now I've developed a new habit of living in these higher energies. Earlier in the process of "doing" this book, there were high peaks. Twenty-one days ago shifting into the energies of spirit seemed like a "high." Now it seems normal. Moving in this spiritual energy seems regular and normal. It's no big deal. Today feels like life has always been this way and will always remain."

"The feeling reminds me of the image of a bird soaring. They just live that way. Everyday they flap their wings and soar high in the sky. It's natural and normal; for they soar anytime they want to and stay high as long as they want. It's the same way for humans living in spirit."

DAY 22

Actions for Today:

1. Write this affirmation 15 times

   I am joy

2. Say this affirmation out loud and pay attention to how you feel. Feel the energy of JOY.

3. Give something to everyone you meet with no conditions attached. It doesn't have to be a material thing; although, it can be. In some situations, you could give a smile, a compliment or a kind word. You could send a positive thought or word to them silently; wishing them love, joy, peace, and happiness.

4. Reflect on today's lessons and write down your thoughts and feelings in your journal.

Today I am Forgiveness

Punishment or Forgiveness?

Sometimes ego's tendency can be to punish people. Punishment can be physical, emotional, and mental. It does not change behavior in the long run. Punishment does not work. It only enables the punisher to do more punishing. Punishment fills the punisher with a "madness" to continue punishing until such time as their awareness heightens and they perceive the harm and ineffectiveness of such behavior.

Let's change the point of attraction to forgiveness which is a powerful energy of spirit. It's like an eraser. Some erasers do the job and nothing is left to be seen of the writing. Other erasers do a job that allows some of the markings to still be seen. Forgiveness has at least two levels.

First, there is forgiveness like a pardon. This would be the erasing that leaves some of the markings. For example, there was a prisoner on death row named Stanley "Tookie" Williams. He was a notorious gangster in California. In fact, he was co-founder of the Crips youth gang as a teenager during 1971. The Crips were responsible for many murders and other crimes. In 1981, Tookie was convicted of murdering four people and lived the rest of his life on death row.

During a stretch of 6 ½ years in solitary confinement and while reflecting on his past choices, he decided to change his life and began to serve humanity from spirit. He dedicated his life to showing youngsters that they have the power to change their hearts and minds, to make a better life for themselves and families. He wrote a series of books *"Tookie Speaks out against Gang Violence"* for elementary-school-aged children to prevent them from becoming gang bangers, ending up in prison, crippled by violence, or killed. The evidence of his good works is the fact that in the year 2000 he was nominated for a Nobel Prize. As his execution date approached many actors and civil activists appealed to Governor Arnold Schwarzenegger to pardon Tookie. The pardon was not granted. In this situation, punishment prevailed over forgiveness.

However, if the pardon was granted his previous crimes would have been forgiven, but not forgotten. The "markings" of his behavior would still be seen because people would always remember and point out that he was a gangster who was pardoned. This is one type of forgiveness.

The second type of forgiveness is when the behavior is deleted from one's record completely and the person is put in an environment where they would never do that behavior again. This second type of forgiveness that deletes the act completely from the record is a forgiveness that comes only from the Source of Forgiveness. The Creator and Sustainer of all is the only One who can forgive like that.

This type of forgiveness may require repentance. There is a story of a man who killed 99 people. He went to a knowledgeable man and said: "I've killed 99 people. Is there any repentance for me?" The knowledgeable man said: "No! Because of those crimes." So the man killed him too which made it 100 people. He continued on his road and found a learned man. He asked the learned man the same question: "Is there any repentance for me?" The learned man said: "Yes! If you will leave this land of bad people and go to another land of righteous people and live with them, then there will be repentance for you."

So the man started on the road to the land of the righteous people. But, he died on the way. Two angels came to claim him body. The angel of torment said: "His body belongs to me because of his crimes." The angel of mercy said: "His body belongs to me because he had repented." G-d sent a third angel to settle the argument. He said: "We'll measure the land between his body and the land of the bad people and the land of the righteous people. Whichever land his body is closest to, then that angel will get his body. The man's body was closer to the land of the righteous people by six inches. Therefore, his body was taken by the angel of mercy and he was forgiven.

Forgiveness is a powerful point of attraction. It feels like a gentle softness that attracts beauty and a gentle kindness. How can you expect G-d to forgive you, who you've never seen, when you don't forgive your brother or sister who you see everyday? Here's a question for you: How powerful would it be if you would forgive people who have "wronged" you? Have they wronged you or themselves? What one does to another, they are doing to their self. Even more so, how powerful would it be if you learned to forgive yourself for your misdeeds? If you would apply forgiveness to yourself, then it would be easier to forgive others.

Give away what you want! If you want to be forgiven, then learn to give away forgiveness to others. Pardon people! Forgive and forget! Maybe in pardoning others, we are pardoned.

Experiences in Spirit

Zayd's notes: "Today was another good day. I didn't do the exercises, but was aware of the energy of forgiveness. Toward the end of the day I thought I should change the exercise to write a letter forgiving myself for all destructive deeds of the past. Next time I'll do that and feel how it goes. It felt good even saying to myself, inside: Zayd, I forgive you for all deeds of the past that were destructive to you and/or others. You are pardoned and forgiven."

One research participant wrote: "Nothing feels more cleansing than forgiveness. Repeating those lines of forgiveness felt like an act of purification that was almost tangible. I was struck by how long and how deep some of my grudges were. One of them drove me to tears

DAY 23

as I forgave the person and myself. I was surprised and upset at how long it had taken me to reach a point where I could choose to forgive that person. I realized how much I had been angry at something as old as my childhood days. I forgave an authority figure whom I love and cherish. I forgave them for angry, impatient behaviors that are now finally behind me. This mix of emotions is strange, but I felt so cleansed and relaxed after I forgave my friends, family, and even a few people whom I know but am not so close to."

Actions for Today:

1. Write this affirmation 15 times

   I am forgiveness

2. Write a list of the names of people you would like to forgive. Say aloud: "I forgive so and so for their behavior." "And I forgive myself for holding a grudge." Repeat these affirmations as many times as necessary until you feel different inside.

3. Contact that person via telephone or a handwritten note. Let them know that they helped you learn some important lessons and you appreciate the lessons you learned. Say thank you. And let it go.

4. Reflect on today's lessons and write your thoughts and feelings in your journal

DAY 24

Today I Am Mercy and Compassion

Judgment or Mercy?

Mercy is the highest energy of spirit. Mercy is full of compassion and graciousness. Mercy is doing "good" for someone even though they don't deserve it. Mercy is pouring out gifts, graces and benefits to others on a consistent basis in a way that may be unseen and unheard. It is done with no desire for repayment. Mercy is saving someone from harm when they are not even aware of the danger.

The Creator is the Source and Owner of Mercy; the One who gives the ultimate of compassion and grace to all creatures. Consider what is done for you, all human beings, and all creatures throughout the universe. The Source of Mercy takes care of every detail of life. Through a consistent and ever expansive, regenerating mercy every creature is provided, sustained, nourished, and comforted. Every limb, tissue, nerve, cell, and organ is operating perfectly. Air is provided. Water is provided. Work is provided. Food is provided. Rest is provided. The heart continues to beat. The intellect continues to function. All of this and more goes on day by day, hour by hour, minute by minute, and second by second because of this quality of Infinite Mercy. This mercy is available to the best and worst of human beings alike. The murderer on death row receives a measure of mercy just as the person who has committed no crime. Praise and gratitude to The Merciful Benefactor who owns mercy, grace, and compassion. All of the praise and gratitude belongs to The Merciful Redeemer who dispenses it with such balance that every creature gets the amount it needs for its situation. Yet, still there is an inexhaustible supply to go around.

If all people could meet in one place and be given whatever they wanted, never would that diminish what The Almighty has as much as a drop of water taken out of the ocean. No human being can be as merciful as the Source. However, can you be more merciful to those you come in contact with daily? How can you extend mercy to your family members, friends, co-workers, strangers, animals, plants, and all living things? You could be a mercy by BEING all of these qualities, energies and points of attraction we've discussed in this book. Demonstrating the energies of spirit daily in behaviors will promote mercy in human life. Suppose you decided to redo this book and practice the process for another 25 days? Would that deepen your journey in spirit? Would that enhance your happiness?

DAY 24

Actions for Today:

1. Write this affirmation 15 times

   I am mercy

2. Decide on one behavior you can do today that shows mercy. Maybe you can say a kind word to someone; give money in charity; leave a 30% tip for the waiter; or write a note to a loved one expressing your feelings for them. These are just a few ideas. What can you do to show mercy today?

3. Reflect on today's lessons and write your thoughts and feelings in your journal.

Today I Am Love

LOVE

All of the energies of spirit discussed in this book are wrapped up in the word LOVE. It is the powerful energy that makes everything go. It is a tenderness that is behind all of these energies. It is a toughness that helps us learn how to be our higher selves. Love is the only thing that exists in the universe. Some of us may have experienced a form of dysfunctional love, but its still love. Everything except love is an illusion created by ego.

Love can be seen in the mother's tenderness with her child. Love is the selfless sacrifice parents make for their children. All creatures exhibit this love. To see an extraordinary expression of love, view the documentary *"March of the Penguins"* narrated by Morgan Freeman. This film is an amazing story of love and mercy. The male and female penguins walk hundreds of miles and go months without food for the chance of having one child. These behaviors are done in the bitterest cold on this planet. Temperatures range from 50 to 80 degrees below zero.

Love is in the design of how creation serves creation. Love is in the sunlight that shines and nourishes. Love is in the rain that falls and ignites growth. Love is in the vitamins and minerals that sustain our lives. Love is a kind word and charity. Love is everything. Love is. You are Love. I AM Love. Love one another. Much love to you! Hope you enjoy your continuous happiness journey.

DAY 25

Actions for Today:

1. Write this affirmation 15 times
   I am love.

2. Share the love with everyone and everything.

3. Reflect on today's lessons and write your thoughts and feelings in your journal.

4. Review your journal entries for the last 25 days.

   Actions for tomorrow: Repeat the 25 day process of living your happiness.

About The Author

D r. Zayd Abdul-Karim known as "Dr. Z" is an inspirational teacher, writer, speaker, and coach. His life purpose is to help others feel better, experience more joy, and achieve their predetermined goals. His daily striving is to bring service, integrity, and spirituality through universal laws to everything he does with people. Through workshops, seminars, and one-on-one coaching, Dr. Z inspires people to live with positive energy and discover new possibilities for being in the world.

For more information on books and services
or to contact Dr. Zayd, please visit
www.drzhappiness.com

Or write to Universal Self-Leadership Institute,
P.O. Box 1946, Springfield, VA 22151